WORKPLACE GEMS

WORKPLACE GEMS

EMPLOYEES REVEAL BETTER WAYS TO COMMUNICATE, MOTIVATE, AND LEAD

JAYNE WITTE, PH.D.

Copyright © 2006 by Jayne Witte. All rights reserved. No part of this publication may be used or reproduced, stored in a retrieval system, or transmitted in any form or by any means, electronic or mechanical, including photocopying and recording, without the prior written consent of the publisher. Only reviewers may quote brief passages without permission.

Examples used in this work are void of specific references to personal and organizational names to protect confidentiality. The author's narratives are based on her unique perceptions of events, and are used to support claims made in the book. Any perceived slights of people or organizations are unintentional.

First printing 2006
Printed in the United States of America

ISBN-10: 0-9778412-5-1
ISBN-13: 978-0-9778412-5-7
Library of Congress Control Number: 2006922409

Published by:
Ladder Climber Books
PO Box 247
Cedar Falls, Iowa 50613-0018
info@ladderclimberbooks.com

ATTENTION ORGANIZATIONS: Quantity discounts are available on bulk purchases. Special books or book excerpts can also be created to fit specific needs. For more information, visit www.ladderclimberbooks.com.

Cover photo by Teresa Tjaden, www.tjadenphoto.com
Cover design by Brian Witte, www.signfusion.com

Acknowledgments

My deepest thanks to:

Brian Witte, my husband, for his patience, support, and good old-fashioned help during every single stage of this exciting and challenging project. You are my main source of inspiration and encouragement, and I treasure you.

Barb and Steve Morgan, my parents, for telling me, from my childhood on, that I could do anything I put my mind to. You support me in so many ways, and I love you.

Steve Jackson, my editor at Ladder Climber Books, for his valuable contributions to the revision process. You give my writing fresh perspective, and I am grateful to you.

The hundreds of unnamed employee contributors, among friends and strangers, audiences and students, for sharing your workplace stories with me. You are the real gems, and this book is for you.

Contents

INTRODUCTION—Eureka!   9

SECTION I—Better Ways To Communicate

<u>The Emeralds In Your Workplace</u>   15
E1. What's On The Feedback Channel?   17
E2. If Perception Is Reality . . .   23
E3. You Got Your Ears On?   29
E4. Talk Is Not Cheap   35
E5. What Is This, The CIA?   41
E6. Stop The Bleeding   47
E7. Let Us Chat   55

Emerald Reflections   59
Emerald Notes   61

SECTION II—Better Ways To Motivate

<u>The Rubies In Your Workplace</u>   63
R1. The Bottom Line Is Not Inspiring   65
R2. You Want More Drive Than Talent   69
R3. Give Us A Reason To Care   73
R4. Where's The Fire?   79
R5. We Don't (Always) Need More Money   87
R6. Is That A Clock Ticking Or A Bomb?   93
R7. We Are Whole People   99

Ruby Reflections	105
Ruby Notes	107

SECTION III—Better Ways To Lead

<u>The Sapphires In Your Workplace</u>	109
S1. Let Go	111
S2. It *Is* About The Coffee!	117
S3. We Are Your PR Department	123
S4. Be Good At Your Job	127
S5. Pick Our Brains	133
S6. Yep, We Are Still Working!	139
S7. Everyone Needs To Row The Boat	143
Sapphire Reflections	149
Sapphire Notes	151
CONCLUSION—Discover More Treasures	153
About The Author	155

Introduction

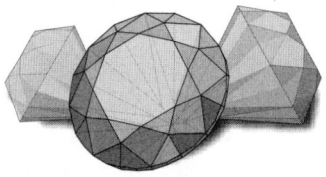

Eureka!

In this rare collection of advice, employees offer 21 ways for leaders to improve the human dimensions of work. Employees want to help leaders create a better workplace that engages, energizes, and enables best efforts. To reach this destination, leaders at all levels should seek inside their organizations to find better ways to communicate, motivate, and of course, lead. The treasures in this book will get you started on the hunt for workplace greatness.

What is in the treasure chest?

Take a look inside and you will find: precious emeralds, to heighten efficiency through interaction; fiery rubies, to inspire excellence through passion; and cool sapphires, to drive performance through guidance.

Each gem in this collection comes with an "action step" you can take right away to put ideas into practice. You could even take a gem-a-day approach to developing your skills. In one month you could become the leader you always wanted to be.

Once you find valuable solutions, spread the wealth to fellow leaders and team members in your workplace. Each section of the book includes a "reflection" segment you can share with others interested in making positive change.

When leaders work together on improving themselves, a renewed workplace emerges where people are more creative, positive, energetic, and productive--pick your favorite adjective(s). Spark a discussion, gather up ideas, and develop workable strategies to move your business forward.

How were the treasures discovered?

It might seem strange, but I watch and listen to people in organizations for a living. In my role as a trainer and speaker, I talk to and gather input from business people in a variety of industries. In my role as a researcher, I experience workers' worlds through first-hand observations, interviews, and surveys. In my role as a professor, I listen to hundreds of front line workplace stories in my classroom. From these three channels of feedback, employees tell me what they want and need from their workplaces.

One day, I had an epiphany. I realized I was sitting on a stockpile of valuable information that could benefit people in all sorts of workplaces. Employees from the service, manufacturing, education, retail, and health care sectors had taught me a great deal about work dilemmas and solutions, but had not been sharing their ideas with their leaders--until now.

I went on a treasure hunt, and collected additional data to round out my existing knowledge base. I began by asking a simple question about leadership to see what employees would say. I asked over 100 employees, "If you could tell your supervisor/boss one thing about how to be a better manager/leader, what would it be?"

Roughly half of the responses focused on communication issues (does that tell you something?), so I developed a separate section for those gems. After this discovery, I followed up with the question, "If you could change one thing about communication in your workplace, what would it be?"

Another one-quarter of the initial responses to the leadership question centered on motivational issues, so I placed those gems in a new section. I then asked a different set of 100+ employees, "What motivates you to do your best work?"

The remaining one-quarter of mixed responses filled the leadership section of the treasure chest. I followed up on certain gems with personal interviews to gather more detailed stories and examples. I also reflected on my own wacky adventures in, and diverse perspectives on, the Land of Employment.

As I designated gems to certain sections, the separation at times felt artificial because these three aspects of workplace life are so deeply interconnected. To be a good leader means to communicate well and motivate often. I cross-reference gems in many places to help you locate valuable linkages.

Introduction

All told, I unearth and display these priceless gems based on employee ideas, suggestions, and yes, even criticisms of organizational life today. Leaders in a wide range of positions and workplaces will learn from the wisdom they reveal.

Who should look inside?

If you are a new leader, this book will be an invaluable resource for you. It will help you see what people want and expect from their leaders. Keep in mind you do not need to hold a certain title to be a leader. Leadership is a particular mindset and a set of behaviors, not a place on the corporate ladder. Employees at any level can "climb" into a leadership role from where they stand.

If you are a veteran leader, you will benefit from the fresh perspective offered here. Many books today are written for leaders, by leaders, but without the input or support from the people they lead. Ironically, we have lost the voice of those being led.

Where, when, and why should I go on a treasure hunt?

Workplaces possess a hidden wealth of information just waiting to be uncovered. To find new gems, you could go low-tech and dust off the good ol' suggestion box. You could go high-tech and use email surveys. You could go the personalized route and talk to people one-on-one or in groups. Collect ideas any way you can, as soon and as often as you can. Workers' perspectives need to be expressed and understood for a business to reach its full potential, because it is employees who hold the keys to innovation and progress.

How do you unlock this potential and lead yourself and others to success? You look in your own backyard and seek the advice of the people who know the nature of the work the best.

Just be ready. You know what they say about finding out the truth--sometimes it hurts. It can also be pleasantly surprising. There is simply no way to know what you will find until you go hunting. Take a leap of faith, be open to new ways of doing things, implement plans, and discover amazing results.

When you embark on a treasure hunt, you will develop your communication, motivation, and leadership skills to the benefit of everyone around you. Before you know it, you will arrive at your final destination: a thriving and progressive workplace. You can begin today by mining the ideas in this book. The rest is up to you.

Enjoy the hunt!

Workplace Gems
14

Communication

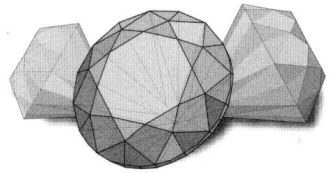

The Emeralds in Your Workplace

Just as the emerald is the most precious of the rarest gem stones, so is communication the most important human process in your workplace. Businesses are in business to make money, but ask yourself: what makes for a strong bottom line? People working together to fulfill customer needs. How does that coordination of effort happen? No other way except through communication. It seems communication is often seen as something nice and fluffy layered on top of an organization like frosting on a cake (*soft* skills, anyone?). It is, instead, the very core of doing business. It *is* the cake, my friends.

Like the delicate emerald, communication should be handled carefully. The *nature* of human interaction in the workplace determines failure just as often as it breeds success. The emeralds in your workplace will put quality communication on your side.

The single biggest problem in communication is the illusion that it has taken place.
—George Bernard Shaw

Emerald #1

What's On The Feedback Channel?

You should be tuned in to this station at all times. Nothing there but static, you say? Then maybe it's time to change the frequency.

In fact, that's a good way to think about feedback--in terms of frequency. We all need it, good and bad, all the time. Do not wait for formal events like performance reviews to share negative feedback or recognition banquets to share positive feedback. We need consistency.

If you wait to share bad news with employees until evaluation time, they will be hurt and stunned. Unintended consequences will follow when employees jump to the bigger questions about your criticisms: "How long has s/he felt this way? Does s/he value my contributions at all?" Upon hearing *unexpected* bad news, people quickly leap to the worst-case scenario--a place you probably did not intend for them to go.

As an internship coordinator, I have had people cry in my office after receiving poor evaluations from their supervisors. The interns felt misled because up to that point, they had received nothing but positive feedback. The rude awakening felt completely unfair.

I understand correcting employee behavior is not fun, and you might be tempted to use the formal processes as a type of protective shield. However, employees want and need you to be forthcoming on a regular basis. An attorney put it this way:

> Leaders should be up-front with criticisms. Do not delay making negative comments for fear of how they will be received. Awareness and understanding of an employer's criticisms are the most constructive first steps toward improving one's work performance.

It may seem strange, but employees *want* criticism--as long as it's constructive! Many people like it when their bosses lay it on the line. A media salesperson suggested:

> I would encourage my boss to be more assertive. It's not that she is dishonest with her employees but sometimes I feel as if she is "sugar coating" things in order to avoid looking too demanding or pushy.

When you try to avoid the "bad guy" label, employees lose respect for you. Interesting, isn't it? Here's why: employees want to make sure their fellow coworkers are "pulling their weight." One theme that comes up repeatedly in the data is that people want quality coworkers who hold up their end of the load. Employees trust that their leaders will make sure equity of labor happens. They don't like it when you let your standards slip for some people and not others (see Sapphire #7). By failing to correct the people who really *need* to be corrected, the employees doing things *right* will become upset and frustrated.

Another possible outcome of avoiding negative feedback is that employees will take advantage of you. They might see you as weak or vulnerable, unable to hold all people on the team accountable. They might decide to break the rules or under-perform, because who's going to stop them? Employees will respect you more when you are direct and consistent with your expectations. When they respect you, they will give you their quality performances.

Now, offering *good* feedback is a lot more fun and enjoyable than delivering bad news, so why don't people do it more often? I think the main reason *all of us* fail to give positive reinforcement is that we are simply wrapped up in the day-to-day stuff so much. People are so busy focusing on their own work that they do not recognize what great things their coworkers are doing.

On the leadership side, some managers may think that employees who do the work well are just doing their jobs like they are supposed to and do not need any positive feedback. Regardless of what you think or how busy you are, the fact remains that if you see a positive behavior that you want to be continued, you must point it out and reinforce it. The behavior you reward is the behavior you get (see Ruby #4).

Problems arise if you wait with good news, too. If the only time you praise people is at an annual meeting or a retirement dinner, they will not believe you! In fact, they will probably be quite cynical about the whole thing. They will think you are saying good things only for the sake of being ceremonial. Good words need to come on a regular, informal, and personal basis. Then when you do speak highly of your people in a public forum, your words will be taken to heart rather than cast aside.

Now, let's not forget the other direction in feedback--the stuff that comes at 'ya! You have to be ready to receive feedback that comes your way, even if the truth hurts. You naturally want to protect your ego (who doesn't?), but you need to lower your defenses enough to hear feedback about how you are doing and how processes are working. Ignorance is *not* bliss!

Do not make the people around you afraid to speak their minds. When employees are afraid to tell the truth, bad news will "magically" get better as it travels up the hierarchy. You will be given a false picture of what is really going on, and a false sense of security to go along with it. The next thing you know, that "little" problem is actually a giant iceberg and you are the Titanic! Stay focused on *what* is being told to you, not *who* is telling you. Employees are often afraid to speak up because they don't want to be shot! (As the messenger of bad news, that is.)

Action Step

Feedback is best received when it is timely, personal, and specific. Do not wait! We need to know *what* we are doing wrong *when* we are doing it wrong. Handle problems when they are still little. Like my doctor once said in reference to symptoms, "Bad things always get worse." Take care of problematic behavior while it is still manageable. The employee can also save face when issues are on the small side. S/he can correct the behavior without feeling embarrassed or devalued.

When it comes to good news, compliment people soon after the event: "Barb, you really went the extra mile last week in designing the brochure on deadline. I'm taking you out for a long lunch at your favorite place today!" (People love food served with their compliments.)

Deliver feedback in person, whenever possible. Not only is face-to-face communication nice, it is necessary to prevent misinterpretation. Face-to-face communication is the "richest" channel you can use, because it has the highest bandwidth for exchanging immediate feedback. It also carries a positive symbolic message. It says you care about the employee and the issue enough to discuss it in person.

Address a specific event as opposed to speaking in generalities. The following exchange focuses on specifics:

> Carl: "I noticed yesterday that product codes were not entered. Was there a reason for that?"
> Bob: "I just thought I would take out that step so we could process orders faster."
> Carl: "I can see how it would be faster, but shipping needs those numbers to keep track of inventory."
> Bob: "Oh, okay, I didn't realize they needed the codes. I'll enter them from now on."
> Carl: "Thanks!"

Compare the above with the following dialogue involving vague feedback:

> Carl: "I've heard you haven't been following proper procedure."
> Bob: "What? Who told you that?"
> Carl: "It doesn't matter who told me."
> Bob: "Well, what procedure, then? I follow the rules."

Carl: "Apparently not, because you haven't been entering product codes."
Bob: "How was I supposed to know? Nobody told me about codes."
Carl: "Just fix it."
Bob: "Fine."

Which conversation would you rather have (if you were Carl *or* Bob)? The key to this approach is to start with a statement of your own (*not* someone else's) specific, timely perception ("I noticed yesterday . . .") and leave it open for the person to explain his/her actions. A neutral approach keeps defenses down.

You need to consistently use feedback to reduce mistakes that affect the bottom line. Meetings are a great time to exchange feedback and reach shared understanding.

Think of feedback as an exchange, a channel on a two-way radio. Encourage others to give feedback (bad news and good news) to you and others on the team. If everyone is dedicated to providing information on the feedback channel, static will disappear, and you will be left with a clear signal that keeps communication strong. Increase the frequency!

Emerald #2

If Perception is Reality . . .
You Better Get Your Eyes Checked

It is quite true what they say: perception is reality. Simply put, how we see the world is the way we believe it to be. In turn, our beliefs shape our attitudes and actions toward those perceptions. (Deep, huh?) Think of all of us walking around with virtual reality goggles on. Everything we see is filtered through these perceptual headsets, and no two are the same.

Basically, it goes like this. We receive stimuli through our five senses, but then we have to interpret it all--fast. There is simply too much information to process, so we take perceptual shortcuts. We expect things will be certain ways based on our past experiences, values, family upbringing, social norms, and so on. A good deal of the time these perceptions are on target, but there are quite a few times when we miss. The trouble comes in the jump between fact and inference.

On the drive in to work one day, I noticed a woman walking on the sidewalk. She was wearing a business suit, and carrying something in her hand. What would you guess it was? My mind quickly put the pieces of the puzzle together. Given the time of day and her appearance, I inferred that she was a professional woman who, like me, was on her way to work. I then surmised that the item in her hand was a briefcase. Imagine my surprise when

I turned the corner to see that she was, in fact, carrying a case of beer! I observed a number of facts about the scenario: female, professional wardrobe, early morning. The rest of my conclusion involved inferences: going to work, carrying a briefcase. Now, those were *plausible* inferences based on experiences and expectations of what "normally" happens (professional people carry briefcases on the way to work), but they were also *wrong*.

We must check our perceptions rather than jumping to conclusions. One of my friends uses an acronym to help her assess situations: FOBFO. It means "find out before freaking out." This handy rule of thumb could be used in a multitude of work situations.

One manager told me that she had an assistant who liked to bring agenda items to the meeting. The manager thought that the assistant was trying to make some kind of power play in doing so. I encouraged the manager to check her perceptions first, before confronting the employee. Perhaps the assistant wanted to be helpful or prepared, or maybe she was trying to help the manager look better. There could be any number of reasons why the assistant did what she did. FOBFO!

When we check perceptions first, we prevent needless (and groundless) conflict from taking place. If you think about it, conflict boils down to a mismatch in perception: I see things one way, you see them a different way, and we argue. But if we stop to check what the other person's viewpoint is before we get caught up in "winning" an argument, we might just find common ground. Who knows? We might even discover that we see things the exact same way.

An engineer suggested that leaders need to check in more often with people at the bottom of the organization to see if perceptions are on target. He reasoned that managers at the top are buffered from certain realities. He said that leaders are often told what upper management wants them to hear instead of what the leaders need to know.

In a traditional hierarchy, people have reasons for protecting their own interests and images. That's why what smells like rotten eggs on the ground floor becomes a sweet-smelling rose by the time it gets to the top. Wrong impressions could lead you to make wrong decisions. You can go on your leisurely stroll of illusion for only so long until you collide with the brick wall of reality!

Another problem occurs when leaders *assume* employees "know" certain things. You might be surprised by how little information they have been given or how much of what they have been given has "sunken in." (I often say that teaching is the art of repetition.) I have heard countless times from managers who do not follow up with their team because they think employees should just "know" what to do and just do it. Yes, they should, after you explain your expectations, provide necessary training, offer feedback, and check your perceptions until you get the result you want.

Finally, people perceive themselves to be good communicators. The truth is, we all have to work at it! I once tried (unsuccessfully, I'm quite sure) to defend my very existence as a trainer to a group of doctors who thought that communication education was unnecessary because it was a "trial and error" kind of thing that had to be learned on the job. One doctor remarked it took him 20 years to figure it all out! (I rest my case.) Just because we get more experienced at communication the older we get, does not necessarily mean we get any better. Our bad habits just become more deeply embedded. Know your weaknesses and take active steps to improve your communication, because you are not as good at it as you think!

Action Step

We have to think about *how* we are perceiving things and take note of when we may be making false assumptions. Be tentative in drawing conclusions. We need to stop before we infer, and consider all possible interpretations. And as with FOBFO, we should simply check to see if we are on the right track.

Recognize your own role in perception. For example, your internal states will affect your judgment. Are you mad, sad, hungry, cold, or preoccupied? Of course, if you really like the person you are dealing with, a "halo effect" can happen where you are unable to make negative judgments about him/her. The "reverse halo effect" operates when you dislike a person--s/he will never catch a break!

Beware of your own biases. True objectivity can never be achieved, so admit to yourself how you might be skewing your perceptions, and adjust accordingly. You might also do well to realize people hold certain perceptions of you that are hard for them to shake.

When I was in sales, I called on an office manager who wouldn't budge: she was staying with my competitor.

She was what you might call a bargain-basement shopper, and I was peddling a high-end product. The interesting thing to me was that her company *prided* itself on making the most expensive product in *their* industry, yet here she was, insisting on cheap, low-quality equipment.

The more I tried to persuade her, the more she dug in her heels. Worse yet, I could tell her attitude toward me turned more sour with each attempt. For the good of my company, I asked that somebody else be assigned to her account, because there was no way she was ever going to buy from me in this lifetime. I felt this adjustment was necessary as I realized her bias against me (and mine against hers) was as stubborn as her buying practices.

With these ideas in mind, here is a quick-reference "avoid" list when it comes to perceiving accurately:

- Avoid early, one-cue conclusions. We all know how strong first impressions are, but try to reserve any judgments until you are able to see the person across time and contexts. See how s/he acts in a variety of situations.

- Avoid ego-centered conclusions. We tend to think, often wrongly, that people's actions and reactions have something to do with *us*. It is a very strong tendency. Mary walks by without saying her usually cheery, "Good morning!" You instantly think, "Is she mad at me? What did I do to her?" Chances are, the lack of greeting had nothing to do with you. She was probably in a hurry, extremely busy, or unable to see you without her glasses on. FOBFO.

- Avoid mind-reading. Again, we tend to think people know more than they actually do. We also tend to think that other people think like we do. Remember those perceptual headsets? Nobody has one just like yours. Do not assume people are on the same page. Communicate until you are.

If you "get your eyes checked," you will not be deceived. Once you have a clear picture of what is going on, you can decide on the best course of action.

Emerald #3

You Got Your Ears On?

You might be tempted to skip over this gem, because you think you are a good listener already. Don't do it! As a general rule, we are all pretty bad at listening. Why? First of all, it is not an automatic process like hearing. People think they can listen just because they can hear. That's like saying I can golf like Tiger Woods because I have two good arms and a set of clubs! Unlike hearing, listening requires WORK and PRACTICE; and as in golf, practice will make you better but it will never make you perfect.

One major contributor to our imperfection as listeners is the brain--it is simply too speedy. We can think a great deal faster than we can speak, so this gives us all sorts of time to think about a bunch of stuff in addition to what the person is saying. Noise creeps in, and we end up pseudo-listening. We dutifully nod our heads all the while thinking about other things like the big meeting coming up, a criticism just received, or what groceries need to be picked up on the way home.

It is the communication skill professionals use the most, and yet are the least equipped to use. We often have no formal training to develop listening skills. Instead, we just repeat the same bad behavior our whole lives (and we have some mighty bad habits, don't we?).

One of the most problematic habits is selective listening. We tune out when we think something is not relevant to us. Therein lies the problem: whenever we *think* something will not be important, that's the precise moment when it will be!

While presenting for the first time at a conference, a colleague of mine started to dread the think-on-your-feet Q&A session that would come at the end of the panel. After the presentations, a voice came from the audience: "I have a question for the first speaker." My colleague was the second speaker to present, so she relaxed. The relief was apparent on her face as she sat back in her seat. In her relaxation, she stopped listening. As the audience member continued with her question, however, it became slowly evident that in fact she was addressing my colleague. Flustered, my colleague sat forward again and tried to mentally catch up with what the question-asker was saying. It was a close call, but she answered the question just fine. I am sure we have all had close calls with our pseudo-listening. Sometimes we are outright "busted" by the person talking, unable to recover from the gaffe or our embarrassment.

Besides selectively listening, we also judge or criticize the person speaking, and jump to conclusions. In short, we evaluate the person and his/her message. While this process is inevitable, it also prevents us from fully listening. Nowhere is this problem more evident than when people are in conflict. When you argue, rather than fully listening to the other person's point of view, you are using the thinking time to craft a response. While the other person is talking you are scheming, "I'm going to shoot back with this brilliant argument and victory will be mine!"

It is also difficult to resist jumping to conclusions when we engage in repetitive communication. A pharmacy technician discussed how she receives, on a daily basis, the same or similar orders from the same assisted living nurse. To complicate matters, the nurse had a tendency of being "short" on the phone. The technician talked about how dangerous it could be if assumptions or judgments interfered with filling prescriptions accurately. Indeed, poor listening can lead to costly mistakes.

Good listening, on the other hand, builds rapport and relationships. Think about the best listener you know. You probably think very highly of this person, because he or she has given you the present of being present with you. This idea of listening as a gift reminds me of Henry David Thoreau's statement, "The best compliment ever paid me was when one asked me what I thought, and attended to my answer." We do feel complimented when someone takes the time to truly listen.

I had a boss who was actually very good at shutting everything else out to listen to ME. He would shut his door, push all paperwork aside, and ignore the ringing phone and the email inbox. The boss would look me in the eye, lean forward, nod his head, and have an expression of genuine interest on his face. Communication folks would say he was showing "immediacy" because he was completely "in the moment" with me.[1] Through his attention, my boss had a way of making me feel like my issue was the only one that mattered. He made me feel important in and valuable to the company--what a compliment! In turn, my trust in my boss deepened, and I gained an appreciation for everything he did for his staff. Compliment returned.

Action Step

Practice active listening rather than passive hearing. You have to work at it. If you are truly listening to something for any length of time, you should almost feel TIRED when it's over. I know I am exhausted after a full day training session, not only because it involves a lot of talking, but because there's a whole lot of listening to do too. When participants speak, I have to process their examples, relate them to previous points, and draw some (witty?) conclusions. You must *choose* to attend to the message. Remember, it is not automatic.

Use the extra brain time to repeat the message back to yourself. You can also paraphrase out loud, back to the person speaking. Make sure you are on the same page on key points before moving on. Ask appropriate questions to clarify and gain more information as you need it.

You can also use verbal and nonverbal back-channeling cues to let the speaker know you are listening. Verbally, these are the "uh-huhs" and "I sees" that the listener sprinkles into the conversation. These cues should be varied in type and should be spaced apart. If you quickly repeat, "yep, yep, yep, yep" I am going to think that you are pseudo-listening or that you want a speaking turn, or both. Nonverbally, the head nod is probably the most common back-channeling cue.

Interestingly, women and men use back-channeling cues differently.[2] I can certainly see it in my classrooms and training sessions. Men look straight ahead and keep their heads still, while women are head-bobbing away!

Women may wrongly think men are not listening because they use verbal back-channeling cues differently as well. When I talk to my husband on the phone, he will often remain silent as I talk. Sometimes I will stop talking just to ask, "Are you still there?" He typically responds with an exasperated, "Yes!" When it comes to verbal feedback, I believe women back-channel to show encouragement to the speaker, whereas men keep silent to show respect for the speaker. Both sexes are supporting the listener with their feedback cues, just in different ways.

Men may therefore find too much verbal back-channeling intrusive rather than supportive, especially when "I see" turns to "Oh, is that Mark the dentist you are talking about?" I think I am being a supportive listener when I pepper the conversation with questions when my husband is speaking. He feels, however, that I need to let him "get it all out" before asking questions. Keep these differences in mind when listening to the opposite sex, and accommodate to the other's style.

Also, try not to judge what you are hearing until you get the whole story. Sometimes the beginning of a comment or argument, if said in a certain way, makes us defensive from the start. From there, we start judging the speaker ("Who does she think she is?") or the message ("He told me about this last month") and we do not give either one our fullest attention.

This goal of "listening without judging" is probably the hardest of all to achieve. We can never completely get rid of this tendency, but by being aware of this evaluation step we can try to do better. Do your best to put the brakes on little judgments as they crop up.

Has it ever happened that once you started truly listening to someone you were having an argument with, you realized you were on the same side? This happened because you stopped judging and started learning about the other person's perspective.

Finally, practice empathic listening. All this really means is that you should strive to be other-centered. Stay focused on the other person's point of view. Put yourself in the speaker's shoes as you listen, and try to understand where s/he is coming from. *Validate* his/her perspective by *listening* to it. Remember how listening is the best compliment we can give? It puts the focus on the other person, and who doesn't love that kind of attention?

If you really must know, being other-centered is the main secret to effective communication, period. So put your ears on already!

Emerald #4
◇◇◇◇◇◇◇◇◇◇◇◇◇◇◇◇◇
Talk Is Not Cheap

Communication is, in fact, expensive. It requires a lot of effort to make it work right. And when it doesn't work right, it costs. The biggest mistake leaders make comes in the failure to recognize communication as the core of everything they do. To overcome this problem, know and live the "3Cs" of communication.

The first "C" necessary to grasp is that communication is *complex*. It is symbolic; it has to be interpreted. It is far more than a means of information transfer; yet, that is a surprisingly common way to think of communication in the world of work. I can't count the number of times I have asked people about communication in their workplace and they say, "Yeah, we have email." That is but a *channel* of communication and it is only one little piece. Yes, we exchange messages back and forth as part of the communication process, but the *goal* of communication is to arrive at a shared or similar meaning between the parties.

And yet, we continue on, thinking that human communication is just like computer communication, where uploads match downloads perfectly, where messages in equal messages out. Within the bandwidth of *human* communication, however, there is a lot of noise going on. There is physical noise, as in the tippity-tap of keyboards going on around you. There is physiological noise, as in the fact that you are hungry, tired, or cold. Then there is a wealth of psychological noise, from worrying, daydreaming, not caring, or not listening. Semantic noise enters when you don't understand the speaker because of unfamiliar words, jargon, or language barriers.

On top of all this noise are relationship issues. Maybe we don't like each other; maybe we are friends outside of work; maybe we just had a fight; maybe I'm interested in you; maybe I'm still mad at the comment you made yesterday; maybe you recently became the boss of me. Whatever stage or dynamic our relationship is in colors our communication.

Finally, we all bring our unique histories, experiences, and values into each and every interaction. My reality is different from yours because we are looking at the world through our own lenses of perception. Given all these variables, is it any wonder arriving at shared meaning is complicated, to say the least?

In communication training sessions, I like to ask the participants to think of a dog. Invariably, people who own a dog think of their OWN dog. Others without a dog still think of a dog they know, either a relative's pooch or one they had as a child, or maybe a famous dog from the movies. Those people who do not like dogs picture a mean face and exposed fangs--hardly the warm and cuddly picture dog lovers call to mind. The word "dog" is just a symbol; people have to fill it with meaning.

Think of this point in the workplace the next time you ask someone to turn in a report "soon." His/her meaning of "soon" and yours is likely to be different. You might mean literally as soon as possible on the same day, while your subordinate thinks a few days or a week is soon enough. And those are just one-word examples. Think about the complicated work conversations you have regarding product launches, customer service processes, employee training, and departmental coordination. Does it still look easy to you? For maximum effectiveness, treat communication as the complex phenomenon that it is.

The second "C" to be aware of is how communication is *central*. It is literally *impossible* to organize without communication. To illustrate this point in the classroom, I put my students in groups and have them build a tower out of nothing but their possessions. I give them no further instructions, except to say that their structures will be judged on height, sturdiness, and beauty. They sit there for a few seconds, stunned, confused, and a little resistant. Then the strangest thing happens. They start talking, and so they start *organizing*. They brainstorm, jump in, try, re-try, negotiate, argue, laugh, complain, build, re-build, delegate, lead, follow, scout the competition, get frustrated, get excited, and ultimately, succeed. It is, from beginning to end, a communication process.

Talk is the main way we figure things out. To function, an organization needs to coordinate efforts toward stated goals. Communication is the central coordinating process, not a tangential or superficial one. Please do not see it as a possession the organization *has*: "We have good communication." Instead, realize how communication *is* the organization: "We are only as good as our communication." The second statement puts communication squarely in the middle of all you do. It literally is the key to business success OR failure.

The third and final "C" to remember is that quality communication is *crucial* to your business. We don't often notice how crucial it is until something goes wrong. My students analyze the Challenger space shuttle disaster to locate communication problems, from intentional and unintentional distortion of messages, to misinterpretation of launch recommendations, to political influences on the withholding of key information.[3]

Another illuminating example can be found by studying the Mann Gulch disaster. Smoke-jumpers were unable to make sense of the chaos surrounding a massive forest fire.[4] A breakdown in communication led to a breakdown in the group's ability to adapt and survive. Several men lost their lives in the aftermath.

These examples, while dramatic, point to the seriousness of miscommunication. During observations I conducted of an emergency room, the nurses told me an interesting story of a pregnant woman who came to their doorstep. The receptionist told the triage nurse that the patient was "in labor." The triage nurse did not perceive the situation to be high priority because "labor" can be a very lengthy process. In reality, the baby was already crowning! The staff said how the woman nearly gave birth in the elevator on the way up to the maternity floor. Notice how the choice of just one little word over another can affect an outcome.

Little missteps and miscues happen all day long, and it is only human nature. But sometimes these mistakes lead to loss of money, productivity, time, and in extreme cases, loss of life. Keep a continuous, close eye on communication to see how it is being interpreted.

Action Step

Work on how you send AND receive messages. The key here is checking for understanding, coming and going. You need to verify that people understand what you are asking of them. In turn, you need to repeat back requests to make sure you understand. Remember communication involves an exchange of messages to arrive at shared meaning. Make sure you exchange enough messages to get there--don't stop short of the goal! We usually crimp our communication because we are in a hurry or because we already "know" what the other person is going to say.

This latter situation is particularly problematic when workers engage in relatively routine communication as part of their job role. Employees in a call center discussed how they receive the same or similar phone orders for product from the same people on a regular basis. They talked about how easy it could be to let something new "slip by" because of the assumption that they already know what's coming.

At a community college, employees noted how they answer the same "frequently asked questions" from students over the phone. The employees said they had to resist the temptation to mentally "skip ahead" to the end of the question. Be sure to listen closely to the sender's complete message and do not assume--you know what happens when you do!

Make sure to work through the noise, relationship, and interpretation issues to see if the meaning received matches the one you sent. On a grander scale, pay close and consistent attention to how your team, department, or organization is interpreting messages, and attempt to straighten out little miscues in the *message exchange phase* before they turn in to full-blown misinterpretations in the *meaning making phase*.

With the sheer *quantity* of communication channels available to us today (email, pagers, voice mail, mobile phones), we need to pay attention to the *quality* of our communication more than ever before. Quantity and quality of communication go hand in hand. Most people I talk to complain there is not *enough* communication in their workplaces, but I wonder how much the problem lies in the *nature* of communication they receive and the *types* of conclusions they are drawing. We need the right amount of messages and feedback (quantity) to bring about accurate shared interpretations of intended meanings (quality).

Know and live the 3Cs and your workplace will be that much better for it.

Emerald #5

What Is This, The CIA?

Don't hoard valuable information. Of course there are certain reasons to be selective about what you share with employees. Just be sure to take a close look at those reasons from time to time. Withholding certain content in the wrong place or wrong time can bring about several possible unintended consequences.

The primary problem stems from the employee perception that you are *hiding* something important from them. There is a difference between choosing not to share information and hiding it. When employees believe you are hiding something, suspicion breeds quickly.

A group of employees shared with me how their upper-level management would gather in a glass-walled room in the center of the office to hold their top-secret meetings. I can just picture all the people on the outside, tip-toeing around that sound proof box, wondering what schemes were being hatched before their very eyes. Apparently the managers would occasionally close the blinds to stop the rubber-necking. Can anything but distrust mount in an environment like this?

In the end, I was told there were no reports that came out of those meetings to the rest of the group; information stayed at the top level.

The trouble with being secretive is that it creates an air of mystery, and mystery creates drama. When you provide people with little or no explanation about goings-on, they will come up with their own version of events. Keeping quiet on a subject will just open the door for others to create their own, imaginative stories that will probably be off the mark. The rumor mill will be in full swing. The drama-lovers will hype up the story as they continue to add in juicy, fictional details. Your molehill will be a mountain in no time!

Added to the mystery is the fact that there is a lot of assuming going on. People assume other departments know what their own department does, for example, when far more often, the left hand doesn't know what the right hand is doing.

When I was a bank teller, I just put my debits and credits into a little outbox. Someone would come around and pick up the contents. For the longest time, I didn't know or care much where they went. I later found out the person used the contents to "run proof" to ensure sure debits and credits were matching. Beyond that step, I didn't know what happened.

Even now, 20 years later, I am far from understanding how the whole of my current organization works. It is so easy to become insulated in our own work, in our own departments. Working at a university, I have people coming up to me all the time asking, "Hey, do you know So-And-So in the math department?" I barely know where the math department *is*, let alone who works in it. Most employees probably have not seen the big picture of their organization.

This is not to say that people want to be left out of decision-making processes that affect them. Particularly in times of change, people want to have a say. In many different businesses, I have heard employees express disgust that they have to go through a change process because management "says so," with no other reason given. If you tell people to change but you offer no rationale for doing so, they are going to resist. But involve them in the change process, and they will support it. If they help come up with the idea, what is there to resist against? When people have a stake in the decisions that have a direct impact on their work, they will embrace change much more readily.

One place where I see people lacking a say in their work is in health care organizations. Decisions are made affecting nursing procedures, for example, but the nurses have no say in the changes. When employees feel they have no control over processes they are responsible for, they will go into auto-pilot mode and just do the bare minimum. They will follow the rules, but their hearts won't be in it. When this happens, burnout is just around the corner. Nursing just so happens to be one of the biggest burnout professions, partly because of the lack of information about and say in their work.[5] And where burnout exists, turnover will follow.

A final, important consequence of a lack of information is costly mistakes can happen. How many times have you heard, after an oversight occurred, "I didn't *know*! Nobody *told me* about it!" An information technology manager could not give a satellite location a fax machine because top management had not shared with employees, for legal reasons, that they were about to be acquired.

What Is This, The CIA?

While the buyout was understandably confidential, no one had told the manager that funds would be frozen for a time. She almost bought the fax machine out of her own pocket because people were thinking *she* was the one who was refusing to fulfill the request.

Intentional and unintentional filtering of information leads to message distortion, which leads to misinterpretation, which leads to problems. Remember playing the telephone game as a kid? It only takes a few people to mess up the message. Now, imagine a single message moving through an entire organization! Passing along messages automatically distorts them, without us even trying. Add on top of this natural distortion incentives to withhold or alter information for political or personal reasons, and you have one big mess.

Action Step

Take a good look at information flow in your workplace. How does it move? Up, down, sideways, in circles? Do your own analysis. Who's talking to whom? How often? What kinds of things do they talk about? Who needs more information? Who needs less?

There exist in any organization informal communication networks. They range from a group of accountants in the accounting department to a group of smokers who congregate outside together, to a group of top executives who go golfing every Tuesday, to the people who swap stories about their kids. All sorts of groups form, and they each serve as sources of information. However, each group will have its own "brand" of information, as each sees the workplace from a unique point of view.

Inclusion in certain groups means exclusion from other groups. If I am a non-smoking middle manager without kids who works in the marketing department, then I will not be included in any of the groups just mentioned.

But exclusion from membership in certain groups can and does lead to missing out on valuable information. Get a handle on how these groups operate and communicate. Once you understand the big picture of communication networks you can locate groups who are not getting the information they need.

Spend some time with employees in different areas, and ask them what their needs are--they will tell you. Look at the quality of information first. Are people getting the *content* that they need? Is the information they are receiving mostly useful or mostly unnecessary? Next, look at the quantity of communication. Some people may feel underloaded with information, while others will feel overloaded. Both conditions, by the way, are sources of stress, so you should try to get it right. Yes, it's a tall order, but if you strike a balance so employees have the right amount and type of information, the easier they can excel in their work.

It is best to be as open and honest with employees as possible, because they are going to come up with their own, fanciful explanations. Not only will these stories be wrong, but will often be of the worst-case scenario variety: "Management just let go a top VP! We are all next. We are doomed!" It is better to remove the doubt.

If certain people are not "in the loop" for certain things, explain why. Simply remove the mystery. If there's no mystery, there's no drama. For example, let's say you delegate an important task to one of your team members. The rest of the team might be thinking, "Why does Erika get that assignment? I've been here longer than her! I do the job better than her!" If you were to explain to your WHOLE team why you picked Erika, then that would end the speculation. You could say, "I picked Erika because she has special knowledge of this new computer program. " Continue with, "There will be opportunities for all of you. Let me know what you might be interested in when it comes to special projects." Mystery gone.

Finally, think about the *symbolic* outcomes of withholding information, even when you have legitimate reasons for doing so. What will people think when you deny access to information? Will they think that you don't trust them? Will they think they are not "good enough" or "important enough" to be "in the loop"?

Employees will read into your communication decisions. Think carefully about how the keeping or giving of information is being perceived and interpreted by others.

Emerald #6

Stop The Bleeding

Ah, yes, the gossip, the backstabbing, the rumors, oh my! The bad news is you can probably never stop these negative forms of communication from happening altogether. (Let's face it; gossiping can be fun . . . until it's about us!) The good news is you can minimize negative communication by not tolerating it and by leading through positive example.

As a speaker, I am often requested to talk about how to deal with "difficult" people--you know, the "black cloud" folks who tinge the workplace with negativity wherever they go. Truth be told, this topic is not my favorite one to address, because there are no easy answers. We can't really *change* anyone else. People have to decide to change, then change. It reminds me of the old joke: "How many psychologists does it take to change a light bulb? One, but the light bulb has to *want* to change!" The most we can do, perhaps, is to shed light on the situation (no pun intended), let the person know how s/he is affecting our work, and hope for the best.

During a training session on motivation, a group talked about how some people just seem impossible to energize. These employees are too busy seeing the glass half empty. A manager in a credit union talked about how he likes to put the ball in the other person's court. If s/he is complaining about a work process or another person, this manager asks him/her to come up with the solution. By asking the employee to take action, the manager stops the cycle of complaining just for the sake of complaining.

If you think about it, much of our complaining is ritualistic. Once we gain entrance into the Order of the Employee, we get a permission slip to complain along with our membership card. It's part of the fabric of organizational life.

I used to have a coworker who loved to consistently bring up a negative point of view on nearly every topic of discussion at our meetings. To the rest of the group, his habit was irritating and seemingly obstructive to the progress of the group. You could see the domino effect of eye rolls go around the room when the colleague would start in on one of his arguments. To him, though, I think his complaining was sport. He loved to play the devil's advocate--that was his role.

I think when we see behavior as ritualistic and not necessarily harmful, we can put it in a better, more tolerable light. In fact, we may actually find some benefit from the behavior. At times, the colleague would make good arguments that would make the whole group stop and think. It's just that he did it so *often* that the group did not have much willingness to listen. It would have been nice if the leader had suggested to my coworker that he pick and choose his battles. If he had done so, he could have had a greater influence on us.

Speaking of groups, we all know misery loves company. When away from the customer and the watchful eyes of management, workers like to get together to gossip, tell stories, mock, joke, and complain. Much of my own research has examined this venting ritual as it takes place in the "backstage" of the organization.[6] What's interesting about this phenomenon is that even as some of the *content* is negative, the *process* of engaging in the ritual is actually quite positive for most participants. It is a way for employees to socialize, learn, and bond as they forge a group identity.

Some organizations try to suppress these backstage expressions because they fear negative feelings might spread.[7] My research has shown, however, that expressing emotion in the backstage is more often helpful than harmful. The ritual helps workers meet performance expectations of customers and managers once back "on stage." The backstage only turns harmful when these sessions take a severe turn toward criticism and blame, when expressing feeling involves tearing down others. So, some venting is good, and is not necessarily a reason to panic. In fact, when we express ourselves, the *positive* feelings come out too!

We need to learn how to express ourselves, as individuals and in groups, in ways that are healthy and respectful of others' feelings, attitudes, and behaviors. One employee in the agricultural lending business mentioned how he does not appreciate it when people "talk down" to others. He reasoned that such behavior was disrespectful to people and debilitating to the cohesiveness of the work environment.

We have to keep an eye on ourselves and others when remarks may be seen as offensive or upsetting to the people around us. The trouble is, some folks may not realize that their attitudes, words, or actions are harmful. We likely have to help each other gain more awareness. We cannot change a behavior we do not recognize.

Action Step

You could try implementing a workplace policy banning such forms of negative communication, but that could backfire. It might just become something else for people to mock and complain about! Probably the best way to handle this type of informal communication is through informal means. Call people out on it and hold yourself accountable too. Lead by example.

I have talked with several employees who say they often "stand up" to negative remarks. They politely request the speaker to stop making such comments. If you decide to confront the "offender" however, one potential drawback is that s/he (and the listeners around them) might make fun of you as soon as you leave the immediate area. But leaders have to be willing to take the heat for trying to stop negative behaviors. For every person who mocks you for calling people out, there will be many more silently thanking you for it.

I saw an interesting trend in the data where employees *wished* their leaders were more assertive in keeping coworkers in line, even if that meant receiving criticism themselves! Some bosses may be afraid of stepping on the toes of the "difficult" person, but others who are impacted by this person are expecting you to do just that. Employees need you to step in because they often feel it is not their "place" to police their coworkers.

As a leader, I look at it this way: if a person's or group's behavior is innocuous, and doesn't seem to be affecting others' work, I leave it alone. However, if I see other people's actions or attitudes are negatively impacted by the behavior, then I think it is my job to take action.

You may need to let your team know they should come to you when a problem occurs. They should not suffer in silence. As a director of an internship program, I put in writing how I want employees to come to me with problems while I can still take any necessary action. I repeat this request frequently.

The key in communicating a problem to the "difficult" person is, in fact, to stay focused on the *problem* and not the person. I like to present the facts in a neutral way, as I see them, and then give the person a chance to explain his or her actions or attitudes.

When I headed up a project involving a committee, there was a member who would mutter to herself when I would explain a new assignment. As best I could hear, she was saying things like, "I can't believe we have to do this project; I can't believe how much work it will be!" I had no problem with the fact that she didn't like the assignment. I *did* have a problem that she was expressing her dislike out loud, and spreading a negative vibe around the room.

After a meeting where this behavior occurred, I pulled her aside and posed a question to her as neutrally as I could: "I noticed today when I talked about the assignment, that you seemed displeased by the requirements. What are your concerns?" As you might imagine, she backpedaled very quickly, and said she had no problem with the assignment; she was just concerned about fitting it into her schedule. As you also might imagine, I never again had a problem with this person making negative remarks.

The key to this technique is referencing a *specific* behavior in a *timely* manner. Using a distinct example gives both you and the other person a clear frame of reference for your discussion. People, "difficult" or otherwise, do not appreciate veiled criticisms like, "I've heard from several people that you have been spreading rumors." Right away, the person becomes upset and defensive: "How many is 'several'? What rumors? How long has this been going on? Do people think I'm a bad coworker?" Refer to something specific, keep your wording neutral (don't assume fault or place blame) and take ownership of your complaint or concern.

A different approach to try involves getting to know the "difficult" person on a more personal level. This advice might be hard to follow because you have likely been avoiding or minimizing contact with this person. What if you went against instinct and moved in the opposite direction, toward spending time with this person? You could find out what the person's REAL issues are in the process.

Usually when people complain, it's about the symptoms they are experiencing. As a leader, you want to get to the underlying problem. That might take a few conversations. Often, the sore spot will be bigger than you thought. The problem usually boils down to fundamental issues of power, control, or respect. If you show the "difficult" person empathy, s/he may open up to you about what is really going on. Then you can get to work at solving the problem at the root cause.

On the group level, you can see collective complaining also as a chance to diagnose problems. Rather than suppressing venting sessions, listen in. Venting is partly a means of bonding, but it can be a means of resisting too--there's something your employees do not like. It could have something to do with customers, coworkers, or bosses. The problem with venting, of course, is the people who need to hear it the most are not present. As a result, things do not change and the venting continues.

Listening in on these sessions is a good way to take the emotional pulse of your workforce: how satisfied are employees with their work? You can tell by the type of venting that goes on. Are the sessions fun, uplifting, and a source of bonding, or are they critical, accusatory, and a source of disharmony? There is usually a tipping point where venting sessions turn from good-natured ribbing to mean-spirited blaming. Do not be afraid of hearing anger or frustration in employee voices. Again, here lie clues to problems that need to be solved.

The truth can sometimes hurt, especially if you find out you are part of the problem! But when you become fully aware of how the group feels, you can then involve them in coming up with action plans that address the *causes* of their concerns. Employees will appreciate having a say in the solutions, and will become more invested in implementing the plans through to success. At the very least, they will value being listened to.

Finally, we need to take a look in the mirror. With all of this talk about "difficult" people everywhere, the odds are pretty good we all have earned that label at some point! Even what we consider to be good behaviors in ourselves could be considered bad behaviors by others. I tend to be direct and to-the-point in my communication, for example. I think for the most part, this trait is appreciated by others, and it works for me. But I can also see where others might think I am being too blunt or harsh, and sometimes take offense to the way I word things.

Sometimes we are "difficult" in spite of ourselves. The leader of a meeting said how he wanted to just make a few quick points and then move on to the main agenda. "Good," I thought, "it will be a short meeting and I have a lot of other things to do today." The next thing I know, I raised my hand and made a comment. It really didn't need to be made, especially given the leader's direction to keep the announcements brief. Well, my comment led to a chain reaction discussion that took a full 20 minutes. I was mad at myself, as were some of my colleagues, I imagine. I was the one who wanted to get out of there, yet I was the one being "difficult"! I brought a lollipop to the next meeting to remind me that I should keep quiet when my comments will not add value to the process.

We need to assess the *outcomes* of our communication from time to time to see how people are reacting to them. If people do come to us with a complaint, we should be open-minded and sensitive to their concerns. We might even decide to *change*, even if just a little bit. Wouldn't that be something?

Emerald #7

Let Us Chat

This request may seem strange but you would be surprised by how many people tell stories about stifling workplaces that do not allow for interaction. An employee in a photography studio said that there were "No Talking" signs posted everywhere. No talking? How are people supposed to function, share responsibility, or solve problems without talking? Sure, her boss was concerned with wasting company time. Take a step back, however, and what appears to be time wasting is actually vital relationship building that will serve people and processes well. We spend more time at work than we do anywhere else. We need those human connections to feel alive and be energized about what we do.

When I was a banquet waitress at a private country club, we had to fold a large quantity of cloth napkins into the ever-popular fan shape. For big parties or weddings, we would have to fold hundreds at a time. Normally, we would sit around a big table and chit-chat about movies, coworkers, and weekend plans while we worked. I remember one time the supervisor came in and, without looking at our progress, yelled, "Less talking and more folding!" Now, I can't chew gum and walk at the same time, but I can talk and fold! The chance to socialize was the only thing that made the tedium of the task halfway bearable.

Beyond the human need for connection, employee interaction just makes good business sense. If people forge relationships with their coworkers, do you know what happens? It's the darnedest thing: they STAY. Research has shown time and again that all things being roughly equal, people stay at a job because of the people they work with.[8] Deny and/or suppress those relationships and you will squash motivation and interest in the work. When that happens, expect burnout, then turnover.

In a workshop on motivation, a middle manager talked about how he had been scolded by his boss for "wasting time" talking to his own employees and trying to get to know them better. He was frustrated, and the rest of the training group was flabbergasted. As a group, we spent the next half hour talking about how he could approach his boss to try and reverse her attitude. I had this sinking feeling, however, that his efforts would fall on deaf ears. We have all been taught that productivity and efficiency are the cornerstones of business. If something doesn't at first *appear* to be productive or efficient, it must be harmful to the organization.

We must reassess what productivity consists of. In part, it consists of talk, valuable talk. The irony of the above story is that the middle manager wanted to get to know employees as whole people so he could better motivate them to work efficiently (see Ruby #7). His boss failed to see he was, in essence, leading effectively through his relationships.

Other benefits of talk include creativity and innovation. If you isolate people and force them to do things that they have "always done" then you shouldn't be surprised if that's what they always do. Get them together and get them talking, though, and creativity springs forth. Like "jamming" in music or sports, people working together can get into a flow state where they reach a whole new plane of performance.[9]

Some of our best ideas come when we are thinking "out loud" or "bouncing ideas" off each other, right? So why in the world would you want to block that creative flow? People learn from *each other* about better, faster, and smarter ways of working. An employee manual will only tell them how it's always been done.

To show the value of talk in innovating, I like to conduct an activity in four groups. Each group is assigned a "manager": one is oppressively authoritative, one is a benevolent dictator, one consults the team but makes a final decision, and the last one is democratic, whereby a final decision is reached by consensus.[10] I then give the groups a scenario: they work in the R&D department of Sunny Morning Cereals, and they are in charge of coming up with two new products. In the two groups with the controlling managers, little innovation is present. They usually stick with something along the lines of bran flakes. In the last two groups, there is far more interaction and openness, and therefore more inventiveness. Groups have come up with everything from peanut butter-and-jelly puffs to a cereal that cures hangovers! The only drawback to these last two groups is that it took them longer to come to a decision. At first blush, it would be easy to judge their processes as inefficient, because of the time investment required. But the *quality* and *originality* of their choices were far superior to the groups with no interaction.

Action Step

Loosen up the reins a little. Give people enough interaction room to forge relationships and hold brainstorming sessions. Will they talk about non-work things along with the work things? Sure. Do you need to panic? No. I have heard stories from part-time employees who had to clock out, even for 30 seconds, if in fact the call they received was personal in nature. Really, in the grand scheme of things, does 30 seconds cost that much? What does it cost if you don't allow some personal time?

Allow employees to at least partially weave in their outside lives within the scope of the work day, and they will appreciate the flexibility. You will also benefit from the *whole* of their personalities being present at work. Employees are more productive in workplaces where they can be fully engaged.

You should understand that an organization is its own little world with its own little culture, customs, language, symbols, and so on. It is a LIFE, not just a temporary space where people focus on the single-minded task of getting work done. Let people LIVE in that space and you will see great rewards come back to you.

Better still, provide opportunities for people to engage in more talk inside and outside of work. Give a group an "imagination challenge" for redesigning a work process or product, for example, where they can meet, discuss, have fun, and flex their creative muscles a bit. You might just be amazed at the results.

Emerald Reflections

The top three most relevant emeralds to me:

1.

2.

3.

Corresponding action plans I will implement:

1.

2.

3.

Obstacles to implementing action plans:

1.

2.

3.

Ways I will overcome obstacles:

1.

2.

3.

Better communication will be evident when:

1.

2.

3.

Emerald Notes

◇◇◇◇◇◇◇◇◇◇◇◇◇◇◇◇◇◇◇

[1] Jones, S. M., and Guerrero, L. K., "The Effects of Nonverbal Immediacy and Verbal Person Centeredness in the Emotional Support Process." *Human Communication Research*, 2001, 27, 567-597.

[2] It has been a long-held generalization that women use back-channeling cues more frequently than men. More recently, it has been shown that frequency does not vary between the sexes, but types of back-channeling cues do. See Marche, T., and Peterson, C., "On the Gender Differential Use of Listener Responsiveness." *Sex Roles: A Journal of Research*, 1993, 29, 795-817, for a discussion.

[3] Conrad, C., and Poole, M. S., *Strategic Organizational Communication*, 5th Ed. Belmont, CA: Wadsworth, 2002, pp. 42-48.

[4] Weick, K. E., "The Collapse of Sensemaking in Organizations: The Mann Gulch Disaster." *Administrative Science Quarterly*, 1993, 38, 628-652.

[5] Putnam, L. L., and Mumby, D. K., "Organizations, Emotion and the Myth of Rationality." In S. Fineman (Ed.), *Emotion in Organizations*. Newbury Park, CA: Sage, 1993, pp. 36-57.

[6] See, for example, Morgan-Witte, J. "Narrative Knowledge Development Among Caregivers: Stories from the Nurses' Station." In L. M. Harter, P. M. Japp, and C. S.

Beck (Eds.): *Constructing Our Health: The Implications of Narrative for Enacting Illness and Wellness.* Mahwah, NJ: Lawrence Erlbaum Associates, 2005, pp. 217-236.

[7] Arlie Hochschild, in her ground-breaking study, *The Managed Heart* (Berkeley: University of California Press, 1983), details how an airline did not want flight attendants to gripe in groups for fear they would develop a negative attitude toward passengers.

[8] Scott, C. R., and others, "The Impacts of Communication and Multiple Identifications on Intent to Leave: A Multimethodological Exploration." *Management Communication Quarterly*, 1999, *12*, 400-435.

[9] Eisenberg, E. M., "Jamming: Transcendence Through Organizing." *Communication Research*, 1990, *17*, 139-165. Also see Kao, J., *Jamming: The Art and Discipline of Business Creativity.* New York: HarperCollins, 1996.

[10] The four manager types come from Likert's (1961, 1967) System 4 Theory, as cited and applied in Pavett, C., and Morris, T., "Management Styles Within a Multinational Corporation: A Five Country Comparative Study." *Human Relations*, 1995, *48*, 1171-1192.

Motivation

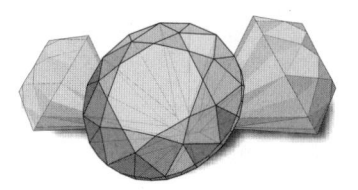

The Rubies in Your Workplace

The ruby, in all its red splendor, calls to mind the natural element of fire; it represents energy, passion, drive, and spirit. Does your workplace motivation represent those things? If not, you need to work to create a motivating space for the people around you. The catch? You can't really motivate someone else to do something. Anybody who has ever tried to get another person to quit smoking or lose weight has discovered as much. But you can give people a reason, a *motive*, for doing their best work.

You can create an atmosphere that energizes rather than drains. You can hire people who are driven, and then make sure to remove obstacles that weaken or kill their spirits. You want fiery, life-giving gems around you, not Kryptonite! The rubies in your workplace will help you create a culture where positive energy flows and passion for the work is contagious.

> *All we need to make us really happy is something to be enthusiastic about.*
> —Charles Kingsley

Ruby #1

The Bottom Line Is Not Inspiring

This statement might be a news flash for you. While the bottom line may consume all of your waking hours (and often your sleeping hours), using it to motivate employees (especially when it is not good) can be devastating to morale. Even in good times, using the bottom line as the sole measure of success devalues the human contributions that went into making that success. Focusing on the end result or product of work lowers motivation because the *process* (blood, sweat, tears) is not recognized as important.

An employee's former boss was brought up in the world of sales. The boss understood quotas, profit margins, and percentages. He didn't understand people. (Notice it was the employee's *former* boss.) The employee, a branch manager, would spend many an evening at work, following up on calls, creating business, and forging meaningful relationships with buyers. He even went beyond his job description to build custom work stations and redesign the retail space to be more attractive to customers. All of this work went unnoticed. And while he did increase sales by a healthy margin, it was never enough; the percentages could always be higher, and come in a little faster. Never mind that the employee's relational style of selling could very well mean more repeat and loyal business in the long term.

A light bulb went off for a training participant when we were talking about this subject. As a sales manager, he suddenly realized that while the salespeople were consistently hitting their goals, he did not praise them, but kept setting the bar ever higher, demanding more without recognizing their accomplishments. He decided then and there to give his people more recognition and pats on the back. The manager realized that he could reward past successes and encourage new ones at the same time. One does not detract from the other.

Sales is a particularly tough business, as I know first hand. When cold calling, I have been thrown out of buildings and threatened (twice) that the police would be called! Self confidence and self esteem take a pounding. It can be difficult to stay after it day after day with quotas that soar ever higher. The over-emphasis on the bottom line by management, then, feels like a brow-beating. It's hard to perform under the added pressure. As one salesperson said to me, "People know what the numbers are and where they stand without the constant reminders."

I worked with a salesperson who had difficulty posting numbers. The verbal lambasting he received from his bosses only made him feel defeated. In turn, he was less effective out in the field. It was a vicious cycle. The more desperate he became for a sale, the less his customers wanted to buy. All the focus on the bottom line can actually backfire on your bottom line.

I remember one sales call I made when I was a representative of a training company. The manager was concerned about sluggish sales and the negative attitudes he was seeing in his people. He wanted me to deliver a three-hour "pep talk" to his sales people, but didn't really want to address any underlying problems. I turned it down (even though I desperately needed the money at the time). I explained to the boss that if he did not get at the source of his team's dissatisfaction, their attitudes would turn even more sour. The salespeople would dislike me and really hate him. Ultimately, he decided to do nothing, training wise. Then he said something I'll never forget: "We have to get sales up first, then we can work on morale." Something told me right away he had it backwards! His comment reminded me of a poster that hung in one of my old workplaces as a joke: "The beatings will continue until morale improves!"

But I think several leaders feel the exact same way about their business: production first, people later. They become so focused on the bottom line that "soft" issues like morale become secondary. But it's the people who drive the business. They need equal, if not primary, consideration.

Putting the bottom line first is a lot like putting the cart before the horse. You have to coordinate efforts toward a common goal that people see value in and can contribute toward (horse). Then the bottom line will follow along quite nicely (cart). What the boss above failed to see is that work gets done THROUGH people, not in spite of them. If you do nothing to nurture and develop people, you will watch your bottom line drop through the floor. Start boarding up the windows, because it is over.

Organizations should be as concerned with people production as they are with product or service quality. Ask the company, "Who are we putting out into the world?"

The Bottom Line Is Not Inspiring

Action Step

Remember to focus on the real motivators. How do people get enthused about a bottom line? Do they leap out of bed and say, "Today I can't wait to increase profit margins by a fraction of a percent!"? Probably not. One retail employee said how her boss in a clothing store told her employees to make more sales so that SHE (the boss) could earn a $1500 bonus! Needless to say, the workers were less than enthused about lining someone else's pockets.

The key is to value all of the hard work that happens in striving toward making the bottom line flourish. You work hard, the people around you work hard. Recognize the *process* in addition to the product. Reward people as they go along toward reaching goals. That's when they need motivation the most!

Think about encouraging a runner in a marathon. Is it more effective to stand behind the finish line and say "Good job" when she crosses or to cheer her on from the sidelines and hand her a bottle of water as she runs by? Now imagine you are the runner. Not only would you appreciate the sideline cheerleader better, you would likely be miffed at the person who simply waited at the end, and rightfully so!

Share your passion for the business with your coworkers and get excited about the process again. When people are enthused about something, they will put their all into the process. Your bottom line will never be higher.

Ruby #2

You Want More Drive Than Talent

When I was in the ninth grade, I was on the C-Squad girls' basketball team. I enjoyed the game. At five-foot-four, I was hardly the star of the team but I handled the ball well and could hustle around the court. There were several guards on the team who were extremely talented and saw the most action. I, alas, was mostly a bench warmer. But I still worked hard, ran fast, and gave my all during practice.

My coach finally decided to reward my efforts with a starting spot for a game. I ran out excitedly and received the inbound pass to take the ball down court to start the game. I ran down the court as fast as I could, my heart pounding a mile a minute. I was not used to the excitement, the pressure, the crowd, the ninth grade boys' team watching, and the *reality* of playing an actual game. When I reached the other end of the court, I stopped dribbling to look for a teammate to pass to. And without thinking, I started dribbling again. The whistle, the call: double-dribble. I was heartbroken, defeated, and most of all, embarrassed. To make things worse, my coach pulled me from the game that very instant so I could not redeem myself. One lousy run down the court and I messed up and I was pulled! In front of the boys! I could have died. Later, my coach said to me, "Jayne, I think you have more drive than talent." I had never been given a more back-handed compliment in my life.

If we really think about it, though, isn't it better to have more drive than talent? Think about all the successful people you know. Do they have more drive than talent? I bet you dollars to doughnuts they do. I'm not saying they are without talent. Of course people must be talented to be good at what they do. But I have known people, and I bet you have too, who have all kinds of talent but don't *drive* that talent anywhere. They aren't necessarily lazy, but they aren't really driven either. And in my opinion, you want the drivers. They are the ones who literally *move* your business from Point A to Point B. Skills can be learned and honed, but drive is something you need to hire for and protect.

You nurture drivers by clearing obstacles like tasks that do not fit their personalities, preferences, training, or experiences well. For me as a teacher, the farther I moved away from the classroom and into administrative tasks and paper shuffling, the more my enthusiasm slipped. Granted, every job is going to have certain aspects to it that are not fun or interesting or even pleasant. As one of my friends likes to so eloquently say, "Every sack lunch has a crap sandwich!"

But I am talking about a more fundamental shift in the work. Newly promoted managers might know this feeling. They were promoted because they did their jobs well, then POOF! The tasks they succeeded in disappear and are replaced by less appealing work.

A man with his own sign business became successful enough to hire an employee. The next thing you know, he was not doing what he loved about sign making in the first place. He wasn't doing the creative, fun work anymore. He was doing the books. This is not why he went into business for himself! Now, of course he had been doing the books when he was alone in the business, but he had the fun stuff to balance it out. In the end, the owner was actually a bit relieved when the employee left to work in another city. Hello again, fun stuff!

As for the ending to my basketball story, my enjoyment of the game slipped away, and I lost interest in supporting the team from the bench. Every year of high school the varsity coach would ask if I was going to go out for the team. Tired of him asking, I finally said something along the lines of, "Why, so you can practice your offensive plays while I stand there like a post?" He stopped asking. The talent I brought to the game, however modest, was gone, along with my passion for the sport. I decided to stick with golf and tennis, because no matter how bad I was playing, nobody could pull me out, and it was up to me and my drive to get myself back on track. I wanted to steer my own course. Most of all, I didn't want to sit out.

Action Step

People enter a certain profession for a particular reason that has to do with an underlying passion. It's important as much as possible to keep that passion at the CORE of the workplace. The core can be multi-faceted, however, so people who come to the work for different reasons can still feel energized. In academics, the core is three-fold: teaching, research, and service. Professors need to perform in all three areas to advance, but can invest their passion more in one area than others over the long term to keep their enthusiasm for the work alive.

When I ask nurses why they chose their profession, answers typically fall into two general categories: they have a passion for taking care of people or they have a passion for medicine, science, and technology. Both of these values easily could be, and should be, incorporated into the philosophy of a health care organization.

Ask yourself, "What are the reasons people chose this line of work and this organization in particular?" If you don't know the answers, find out. Then create a gem-like core (multi-faceted, get it?) that reflects those reasons. Publish this core and make it known, then protect it. Remind people often of why they signed on for your business and how you intend to keep the core going strong.

As a leader, you want more drive than talent on your team. You want the spark, the enthusiasm, that drivers bring to the game. Please don't bench 'em.

Ruby #3

Give Us A Reason To Care

The secret to motivation lies in the connections. If people feel connected to the customer, their coworkers, or the organization in general, then they will give a darn.

I once gave a talk to city employees. During introductions, one man sheepishly said, "I'm just a garbage man." Just a garbage man? I asked all of the city employees, "Do you know how valuable your service is to this community? What if there was no garbage collection? No police? No library? No utilities? The city wouldn't be able to function!"

If you take a customer-based approach to motivation, then every job becomes important, every person has an inspirational task to accomplish that means something to the bigger picture, and every team can work together to fulfill customer needs. When this happens, expect amazing results.

As I gathered data about motivation, I realized people truly *like* their customers; they like serving them. I think because I have worked in many service jobs dealing with a demanding and sometimes angry public, I first found this trend in the data to be surprising. The more I thought about it, though, the more it made perfect sense. How the end user benefits from what we do is the true measure of our success.

During a training session, I asked people what they liked about their jobs. At first there was a big pause (cue the crickets chirping). I thought, "Oh-oh, this isn't a good sign!" Slowly, they began to speak. All of their answers reflected helping the customer--solving their problems, making their lives easier, better.

My husband worked for a printing company that created blueprint books for contractors bidding on commercial jobs. On one particularly big task, I offered my help. I was on the binding machine, inserting materials and punching out plastic combs. Soon you could hear the "KER-CHUNK, KER-CHUNK" sound of my progress. Tedium set in pretty darned fast, and I wanted to quit, overwhelmed by the giant stacks of books that needed to be bound. But then I took a closer look at the building being depicted in the books. It was going to be a strip mall with a couple of my favorite stores in it. Suddenly I became much more enthused! The contractors *needed* me to do this for them. Without ME, this building would not be built. I also wanted to shop there when it was done! The ker-chunking sound came fast and furious.

People also need to make connections to others *inside* the workplace. One interesting finding in the research is that when people care about the people they work with, they will care about the company and its goals in turn. Volunteers in a nonprofit organization, for example, have a higher likelihood of staying with the organization if they have positive relationships with their fellow volunteers.[1] Connections to the work are made *through* the people we work with. This link, once made, is an incredibly powerful force in your workplace.

I conducted training for a company who consistently provides ways for employees to form a bond. Some of these opportunities are formalized, others just happen. They sponsor events that encourage healthy habits, from hosting in-house weight loss programs to giving prizes to people who walk a certain number of miles. One of the employees won a weekend trip for two to a luxury resort. The company also hosts outings and parties, including a tailgate at a football game.

Informal activities have also become part of their culture. Employees formed a team for a kickball league, and wore neon green shirts to enhance their team spirit. A group of women in the company started "girls' night out" events. In the summer, they go golfing every other week. What's interesting to me, though, is how the company supports these informal endeavors, even though they did not originate from management. For example, the golf group was given golf tool kits and towels with the company logo on them. Pretty cool!

We spend more time at work than anywhere else. We spend more time with our coworkers than we do with our families and friends. It is highly motivating, then, when people can forge positive relationships at work.

Action Step

Giving people a reason to care involves helping them make connections to others inside and outside the workplace. No matter what we manufacture, process, and sell, we are all in the people business. At the end of the day, we do the work with people, for people.

At a professional women's group meeting, we were asked to each write down what motivates us. I jotted down the answers from my table:

- Coworkers, people
- Customer focus: treat like a friend, take care of them like family
- Work hard, play hard--enjoy family nights and weekends
- Like to learn, delve into something new
- Building people up--customers and employees

I think this list says it all. It shows how important connections are to people. It also shows how people make *different* links to what motivates them. Five people sitting around a table can have five different reasons to care. That's okay! It just reminds us that people are motivated by different things. What makes the items on this list similar, though, is the connection to *people* in our work and personal lives.

In my research, I have found that people use many different sources, located both inside and outside of the organization, to make a connection to the company.[2] Customers and coworkers remain two of the main sources employees use to identify with their companies. When workers feel a connection to their organizations, they are motivated to *perform* and to *stay*. In my study, some employees talked about how they "bleed" the company colors. Talk about a deep connection!

To develop customer-based motivation, help people see how their work plays a role in the big picture, and emphasize how customers' lives are improved as a result.

This process may take several steps. An engineer of a manufacturing company had a harder time of making the customer connection than other attendees in a motivation training session. His company made parts. These parts were sold to other companies who made machines. The machines were sold to other companies so they could make the product. For the engineer, the customer was a long way off in the distance! I pressed him about how the end user would be affected if he *didn't* make those parts. "For one thing," he said, "People wouldn't be able to use toothpaste!" Among other things, his parts helped machines fill the tubes with the cavity-fighting stuff we all need every day. Even if your team is far removed from customers, help employees take the steps to see how their work is important to the end user.

To develop the coworker source of motivation, the first step would be to, of course, hire good workers who will "pull their weight." I have found it is very important to people to have quality coworkers (see Sapphire #7). Beyond the hiring step, be sure to provide ways for people to bond and have fun together. In a company I researched, a few people lamented how they missed the "old days" of when they were more like a "family." They mentioned how there used to be softball games and company picnics, but no more.

The goal, then, is to either provide planned get-togethers for people, or let ideas and events develop naturally through employee interaction. Then, don't stand in the way or, heaven forbid, nix events after they have been established. People become very attached to their softball games and, by extension, their coworkers and, by further extension, their company.

Give Us A Reason To Care

Finally, do not underestimate the power of symbolic identifiers like logo T-shirts, coffee mugs, and so on. These items, while not so good as items of recognition, *are* good for building a group identity. Some employees at a manufacturing company talked about how they wished they could have embroidered jackets like they had in the past. People like to feel proud of where they work. They want to feel a part of things. They want to be identified with the company, especially if its public reputation is good.

It may seem silly, but my volleyball team went from a ragtag bunch with a losing record to a highly unified team of winners once we had a name ("Lightning Spikes"--I thought of it!) and matching shirts (a flaming volleyball on purple tie-dye--very cool!). The emblems helped us feel like a team, and so we started acting like a team.

When people feel like they *belong* to something special or successful, they will be motivated to perform. In a word, they will *care*. Then they will excel.

Ruby #4

Where's The Fire?

Let's face it, a big part of a manager's job is to locate and fix problems. In fact the word "manage" implies that something unruly needs to be controlled. So, it becomes very easy to stay in problem-detection mode, fighting fires. Unfortunately, this behavior wears thin on employees. They would like you to switch gears once in a while, to spend some time in achievement-detection mode, lighting fires (of motivation, that is).

As a professor, a big part of my job is to be critical of my student's work. When it comes to grading, I splash plenty of red ink on the pages. After all, I am looking where points are coming off, not where they are going on. I suppose that is the problem with most motivational systems companies have in place today: they are punitive rather than rewarding in design.

A salesperson, while reflecting on a previous workplace where management always kept an eye out for bad behavior, exclaimed, "They treated us like first graders!" She said that salespeople were told a story of how the company hired a private detective to spy on an employee. According to the story, the employee was fired when it was discovered he was wasting company time, doing non-work activities out in the field. The story carried a not-so-subtle warning to the rest of the workers.

The salesperson told me she was afraid to even pick up her dry cleaning when she was out making calls for fear that a PI would be lurking. Of course, this reaction was exactly what the company wanted! But breeding fear, while perhaps powerful, is not the best way to motivate people for the long term. When you breed fear, you breed resentment right along with it.

I remember being told a similar story when I was in sales. One employee had been "busted" taking too long of a break. The story had us believing the manager barged in to the employee's house to see him sitting on the couch, watching TV, and eating lunch well past the noon hour. Another story I heard was of a woman who was "busted" working out at a health club during the work day. The irony was that the manager who "caught" her was also there to exercise!

Stories in organizations are told as a type of moral or lesson for people to heed.[3] The story provides some distance, so management isn't telling you "directly" what to do. They would rather create an atmosphere of paranoia, I guess! Now, I am not suggesting that it is wrong to have some guidelines about what employees should or should not be doing during the work day. But I think it is best to explicitly state what those expectations are and then believe people will follow the rules.

When I ask employees from different organizations what motivates them to do their best work, the number one response involves positive relationships with coworkers. The number two response? Praise and recognition. The salesperson mentioned above noted how kudos are cheap--cheaper than the "trinkets" of recognition that management often hands out! She said she didn't want to be given a token but instead be told, "We want you here." The little praises mean the most, and are indeed free.

When I was consulting with a group of managers in a department store, they wondered aloud how they could reward employees. They brainstormed ideas like giving an "employee of the month" a plaque, coffee mug, or parking space. I spoke up and said, "How about telling employees 'Thank you'?" I received some very strange looks, like that little phrase couldn't possibly be nearly enough. If sincere gratitude is expressed on a regular basis, though, it can easily be enough thanks.

We all know an expert lives 50 miles away, so sometimes we fail to recognize all the talent people in our own organization bring to the work. A salesperson didn't find out he was a star performer until he went to a company-wide conference. People came up to him and said, "Wow, I have heard about you!" His immediate supervisors gave him no indication he was doing so well. He said they get tied up in nit-picking on little things he might be doing wrong as opposed to rewarding his overall accomplishments. His bosses failed to see that lighting fires (with recognition) rather than fighting fires (that don't really exist) would further ignite his performance.

Action Step

Work from the assumption that people are doing things right rather than messing things up. Employees can tell the difference in your mindset! Your good employees will not appreciate being lumped in with the bad. Single out the low performers as needed, and leave the high performers alone. Do not make veiled threats or blanket punishments: "*Everyone* needs to fill out performance reports or be fired!" Identify people who need guidance to get back to the standards you set, and help them out. On the other hand, recognize and reward good work done by good workers.

Work that is rewarded is work that will continue. The key in providing recognition is the same as providing feedback (see Emerald #1). Praises should come in small, frequent doses that refer to recent, specific incidents.[4] Compare the following options:

> Choice A: "Todd, you did an excellent job compiling and editing those reports. You sure put in a lot of extra hours to meet the deadline yesterday. Because I know you love to collect movies, here's a $20 gift certificate you can use to buy a DVD!"
>
> Choice B: "Good job, Todd. The reports are finally done. I can always count on you." [Slaps Todd on back.]

Maybe Choice B doesn't look so bad standing alone, but when compared to Choice A, it doesn't hold a candle. Why? Look at the elements. The recognition in Choice A refers to a recent, specific accomplishment--the reports done yesterday. And while Choice B refers to the same thing, it does not mention specifically what Todd did for the reports. It only refers to the outcome, not the *process*. The process is where all the work went! The *effort* needs to be recognized along with result.

Then Choice A takes it one step further: it personalizes the reward to something Todd likes. People enjoy recognition far more when it is tailored to their likes, interests, or personalities.[5] The "I can count on you" remark in Choice B likely makes Todd think he will only be "rewarded" with more work! To make matters worse, Todd could find the slap on the back trite and condescending.

Make sure the rewards you give out match the achievement you are attempting to recognize. I was excited to go to a tenure and promotion luncheon on campus. I had earned T&P (industry term) earlier that year, and was looking forward to being recognized by my peers. It was a major accomplishment that required five years of enormous effort, as I dedicated myself to researching, writing, publishing, teaching, and service.

My excitement dimmed, however, when I was told I could not bring my husband to the event. I received an email along the lines of, "As much as we know how your family is proud of you, we can't afford to have family members present." Couldn't afford it? The luncheon literally consisted of a salad and a piece of cake. There wasn't even an entree, for Pete's sake! I reached one of the biggest milestones in my profession, and they couldn't afford for the most important person in my life to take some more lettuce out of a bowl or take another slice off a sheet cake?

At the luncheon, I noticed a pile of gifts wrapped in shiny gold foil. My spirits rose again, as I felt like a kid at Christmas. I figured something great had to be in there! When I was back in my office, I ripped off the packaging with great anticipation. I deflated again when I opened the box to find . . . a lousy key chain. It was a faux copper thing that was probably no more than $2.95 in the bookstore. It was ugly, and I was tempted to throw it away. As my only reward for tenure and promotion, however, I thought I should keep it. I threw it in my desk drawer, and haven't looked at it since. I rather would have received a nice plaque or even just a paper certificate in a frame--*something* to hang on my wall that tells the world, "I did it"; *something* that mirrored the achievement.

Keep in mind that people are also a source of reward. The only saving grace of the luncheon was that my department head was there to support me. I know he was busy and probably had a million things to do that day. But he came to my luncheon and sat at my table. Just his presence spoke volumes.

The only word of caution with reward programs of any kind is to be prepared, in terms of effort and resources, to keep traditions going. Once started, these programs carry a symbolic significance for people, and employees will become attached to them. If programs are removed or stopped before they have run their course, then employees will be more upset than before the program began.

You no doubt have heard the expression, "It is better to have loved and lost than to never have loved at all." This statement does *not* hold true when it comes to incentive or reward programs! It is better to receive no recognition at all than to have had it for awhile and then taken away. In one workplace, the "Employee of the Month" plaque was three *years* out of date. Oops. What symbolic message did that send to employees? You have to keep lighting fires all the time for motivation efforts to be successful.

Amazing things come back to us when we do take the time to reward others' work. One day, I was grading an excellent student paper. On any other day I may have just put an "A" on the paper and been done with it. But this time, for some reason, I wrote something to the effect of, "If you want to present this paper at a conference or send it off for publication, I will help you."

The student took me up on my offer. She and I spent the next year and a half getting it ready for publication. Talk about a huge investment of time and energy! A communication association held a student paper competition. The top prize was a presentation at the conference and a publication in their journal. She won. The student was so thrilled and grateful; it was a remarkable experience for both of us. Even though it was a big commitment on my part, it was one of the truly inspiring moments of my career.

Going the extra mile for someone else, while effortful, can be very self-fulfilling. Motivation is contagious. When we light fires in others, we light fires in ourselves.

Ruby #5

We Don't (Always) Need More Money

Find out what's motivating to people. As a knee-jerk response, most people will say, "Money." But when people do ask for more money, look at the reasons why. Is it because they can't support their families, or is it because they are feeling unfulfilled and/or undervalued?

Some leaders may think money is enough to make people happy. In return, they expect people will do their jobs to their fullest, simply because they are getting paid to do so. However, studies have shown that money, as an external reward, is not the greatest long-term motivator.[6]

We are initially concerned with money when we are first hired, but once we have achieved a certain amount of security in the job, it slips in importance. If, on the other hand, we do not have enough to meet our living requirements, then it becomes an all-consuming issue. When you have enough money, you are like a fish in the water. You don't even think about the water; you probably wouldn't be able to define "water." In contrast, when you don't have enough money, then you are like a fish out of water. All you can think about is getting back into the water--FAST! It becomes your number one priority, because your very survival depends on it.

Therefore, people want to be compensated appropriately and fairly for the work they do. Once that step has been achieved, however, they focus on other things that bring them work satisfaction. What do they want?

Among other things, people want to . . .

- contribute to something bigger than themselves
- make a difference
- connect to their work personally & emotionally
- feel appreciated
- engage in challenging work
- have positive, rewarding relationships

There is no single path to motivation. You have to find out what makes people tick.

Not surprisingly, in one of my sales positions, the focus was on money. More specifically, the motivation was based on what money could *buy*. My bosses told us to cut pictures out of magazines of luxury items that we wanted. And we were supposed to think big--sports cars, yachts, mansions, hoity-toity watches, and so on. My bosses were even proud of their very expensive pens! (I carried a basic ballpoint.)

We were to take these pictures and put them on the visors in our car. Then, right before we went in for a sales call, we were to flip down the visor and look at the picture. We were supposed to find it motivating. Because my bosses were motivated by the acquisition of status symbols, they thought everyone would be.

It's a common mistake. People are successful in their work and they are promoted to management. Naturally, they are going to think their strategies will work for other people too. Unfortunately, it doesn't always work that way. I was more of a goal-oriented person. I figured if I met quotas, the money would follow.

When people do not find sources of motivation that work for them, they might be headed towards burnout. Watch for symptoms in coworkers. Do they feel like a failure, see people and processes in a negative light, or feel like they can't face another day on the job?[7] Find the root cause(s) of discontent.

People lose zest for the work when they are unable to bring their strengths to the table. I remember being stuck in a job I did not like. The routine of it all was getting to me. I talked to the job counselor from the employment agency who placed me. She said I should do creative things outside of work to fill the void I felt at work. At first this notion made sense, but then it got me thinking: why reserve our creative strengths for use outside of work? My employer and I both lose.

Who has the time and energy to really pursue those creative passions *after* work, anyway? Employees have already given the most productive hours of the day to the organization. It is difficult to use the precious few hours left in the day to paint, write songs, knit, golf, or whatever, when the bulk of that time is spent preparing food, eating, feeding others, cleaning up food, and washing food off clothes. Generally, we spend our free time getting ready for the next work day. There really is no choice but to invest our creativity during work hours.

Yes, there must be a good job fit up front. In my example above, I was not a good fit to begin with, and I should have self-selected out of the organization a long time prior. I wasn't serving anybody there, least of all myself. But if the job is a good fit in general, then employees and leaders should work together to tweak the roles in a way that best suits the workers and the workplace.

A skilled leader can find ways to spread out work according to people's interests and strengths, regardless of job titles or descriptions. Jump over "not my job" hurdles to reorganize tasks and folks as necessary so that you have as many win-win situations as possible.

Action Step

What do people want? Ask them, they will tell you. Then customize your motivational approach accordingly. Some people are goal driven, others crave recognition or bonuses. Mostly, they want to make a difference, to contribute to something meaningful. Find ways to make that connection for EVERY job that is under your leadership. There is meaning and value in each one, but you may need to help your coworkers see how their contributions matter to the overall success of your department and organization.

If you think people are headed toward burnout, be sure to get to the root causes fast. As one employee told me, managers are not always aware of all the "pressures rolling down hill" from the top of the organization. She talked about the snowball effect that would happen when one VP, unaware of her constraints, would add to the demands another VP put on her, and so on down the line. The burden gets larger and larger to manage. Take action on the *cumulative* workload employees experience.

Be aware of and destroy spirit killers--people and processes that zap the energy out of folks. Address spirit killers head on.[8] On the process side, when you eliminate needless paperwork, for example, people will feel like a great burden has lifted, and their spirits will rise right along with it. On the human side, if you have a toxic person in your workplace, you have a responsibility to the other members of your team to curb his/her behavior (see Emerald #6).

I suggest leaders take the CLEAR path to motivation:

- Communicate—you have to let other people know what your needs are so they can offer you their strengths.
- Learn—get to know the people you work with so you understand their work styles and motivational preferences. One employee told me that her two best bosses took her out to lunch one-on-one to specifically achieve this goal.
- Empathize—No one is able to be "happy" and "productive" or "give 110 percent" one hundred percent of the time. When you understand another's point of view, then you can see why s/he may or may not be motivated at certain points in time. Stand in coworkers' shoes once in a while to gather and validate their perspectives. People have good reasons for feeling and acting as they do. Sometimes, you have to give them a break from being "happy."
- Ask—Again, people will tell you want they want if you only ask.
- Recognize—Reward behavior that you want to see continue. Follow through on incentives and say thanks for jobs well done.

We Don't (Always) Need More Money

Many employers would benefit from this CLEAR path to motivation, especially those who think money is the only answer. It is ONE answer out of many possibilities. As we all know from looking at our bank statements, money only goes so far. So, too, does the motivation that comes with it.

Ruby #6

Is That A Clock Ticking Or A Bomb?

Sometimes people, both hourly and salaried, are fighting the clock. Remember those big clocks in elementary school? (Well, they seemed big then.) Instead of a regular tick-tock sound, the minute hand would announce its slow progression with a loud THUNK. Sometimes, it feels like that at work. And when people use the clock as a motivator (as in, "Only twenty more minutes and I am outta here!"), their hearts will not be in the work. The problem is made worse when managers encourage the use of this not-so-good motivator, intentionally or unintentionally, through their actions.

When I was in sales, I had two bosses, both with military backgrounds. "Discipline" was their middle name! And they had big issues with time. If I happened to walk in the door at 8:02 a.m., they loved to say, "Good *afternoon*, Morgan!" (Morgan is my maiden name.) I felt like the newest recruit rather than a valuable employee. Punctuality is a virtue, but counting the minutes takes it too far. Apparently a number of us were coming in two minutes late, because my bosses moved the official start time of the business day back to 7:30 a.m.

They also watched us like hawks at the end of the day. One of their favorite expressions referred to an action by cartoon character Fred Flintstone.[9] When Fred was at work, he would slide down the dinosaur tail right at

5:00 when the whistle blew. If I left, say, at even 5:30 because I had a haircut appointment or simply because I was done with work, they loved to say, "Sliding down the tail again, huh Morgan?" So, most of us stayed until at least 6:30 just because our bosses thought we should. It was face time, pure and simple. I don't think it did a darned thing for our productivity, but it kept our bosses off our "tails."

Now, I'm not saying discipline is a bad thing, but neither is a little flexibility. More and more workers are looking for employers who can be flexible with time. They are going to seek out and stay with companies who focus more on work done than time spent.

There has traditionally been a focus on quantity in our nation. From the dawn of the Industrial Revolution there has been an emphasis on output, speed, efficiency, and number of widgets produced per hour. And these are all desirable things. But in an information age, and even in the widget-maker's house, quality needs to hold an "equal to" or "greater than" place to quantity. Look more at the *value* that comes out of the work, and not so much the time that goes into it.

The truth is, we make a lot of assumptions about time, and how people spend it. As in my own work example, the notion of face time, arriving early and staying late, is highly regarded in some workplaces. You apparently tell people that you are a "go-getter" when you put in the time. On the other hand, you are considered a "slacker" if you arrive late or leave early. People use the clock as evidence for these judgments.

But just like any other assumption we make, we have a 50-50 chance of being wrong (see Emerald #2). Perhaps that go-getter is actually a workaholic who is neglecting other areas of life, or is a slacker-in-disguise, putting up a good front for the boss. Maybe someone who is there for a shorter time is simply more efficient, or plans on taking work home. You never know.

A manager in a medical equipment business realized that she had been making a poor assumption of one of her staff members. She was thinking the employee was a procrastinator because he always turned in his work at the final buzzer. It wasn't late, just right at the deadline. Giving this more thought, she concluded, maybe he's actually managing his time and projects better than the rest of her staff! Maybe the rest of the staff made the project a priority when in fact other things should have come first.

The moral of the story is, move deadlines according to when you actually need them, and then do not be upset if people take the whole time to meet them. In my experience, most people will take exactly as much time as you give them. It's a human nature thing.

Another main belief about time is that we have to be "busy" to be productive. Again, this idea is over 100 years old in our nation's work ethic.

When conducting observations in a cardiac catheterization center, I noticed how the nurse manager would tell the staff to "look busy" when the cardiologists (who happened to own the place) would stop by. Now, it's not that the nurses were lazy. It was just that, at times, there was literally nothing to do. They were efficient enough to be caught up in their work until the next spurt of activity would come about. However, if one particular owner saw people "standing around" during a slow time, he would exclaim, "What am I paying all these people for?" Again, the assumption is busyness = business.

An employee who works in a warehouse for a beverage distributor said he likes to hustle to finish his assigned workload so he can relax and take a bit longer of a break. But when the boss comes around and sees him on his well-earned break "doing nothing" he scolds the young man for being lazy. Of course, the opposite was true, but it didn't *look* like he had been busy. Had the boss not rushed to a conclusion, he might have rewarded the employee's productivity.

Action Step

The first step is to identify any clock-watchers in your workplace. Who is using the clock as a motivator? Help them re-evaluate their work, to see if their talents are being used to the fullest. If not, add something more challenging or interesting to their work lives. Think about your favorite pastime, game, or hobby. When you are engrossed in something you truly enjoy, time becomes a non-issue. It's true what they say about time flying!

Second, we have to remember that people often have good reasons for using time as they do. Sure, if a situation is a chronic problem that affects other people's work, than address it. But otherwise, give people the benefit of the doubt.

We become hyper-aware of people's comings and goings, but where does this get us? We can be very critical of others without knowing the whole story. So when you find yourself making assumptions about other people's time, stop, and check your perceptions. Ask, *in a neutral way*, about the person's time usage, if it is in fact important for you to know the reason. If it is not really important for you to know the reason, drop it and focus on your own time management.

Finally, you should be most concerned about the *quality* of the work and whether it is meeting *objectives*. Ask yourself what end results are required, and if people are achieving those ends. Simply put, don't become so wrapped up in the tiny stuff that you miss the big picture importance of the work (see Sapphire #6).

If I close a big sale today, does it really matter if I walk in at 8:02 tomorrow? Most people expect and need a certain level of accountability, but be careful not to go overboard. Make your expectations and standards known, and certainly set them high. But then give people some breathing room in getting there whenever possible (see Sapphire #1). Do not get too hung up on the little details, or make assumptions about the different routes people take in accomplishing tasks.

Reward people with flexibility, and they will reward you with their talent, energy, and yes, time.

Ruby #7

We Are Whole People

People want to feel valued and understood as whole people, not as role-fillers and certainly not as cogs in a machine. When we are so busy, it is easy to see people as their positions (salesperson, marketing guy, computer wiz). I have to catch myself doing this when I am in high task-drive mode. But as much as possible, we have to remember to treat coworkers as well-rounded, complex people who have a life, families, and a complex system of thoughts, beliefs and talents that is only partially shown at work.

One workshop attendee, after discussing this topic, suddenly realized she had been calling her teams "the night shift" and the "part-timers" and was failing to recognize them as individuals. She decided at that moment to get to know employees better. In the data, when employees mentioned what they found motivating in a boss, they overwhelmingly answered, "When s/he understands I have a life." Employees want to be understood and valued as whole people who bring their whole selves to work every day.

Part of seeing the whole person is seeing the emotional side of the person. A lot of workplaces want us to check our emotional selves at the door; we should be rational, logical beings at work. Of course, we are rational, but we are all emotional too--all of us.

Maybe you have heard someone say, "Set aside your emotions to make a good decision." Instead of suppressing emotion, we should tap into it, channel it, and use it to guide our rational choices. When there is tolerance or even celebration of human feelings, people feel more fulfilled at work.

One employee in the printing industry reflected on how her favorite bosses took the time to find out exactly how she preferred to work. They asked her about her interests and motivations. They asked her, specifically, how she approaches work and how she likes to get the job done.

The employee noted how talented these bosses were for being flexible enough to adapt their styles *around* employee preferences. This idea is quite foreign to most bosses and indeed, most organizations! Usually the reverse happens. Procedures are usually well "spelled out" long before an employee comes on the scene, and s/he is simply told what to do. In the above organization, however, processes were designed by employees. How could people not be motivated to excel in systems that they customized to their liking?

Action Step
◇◇◇◇◇◇◇◇◇◇◇◇◇◇◇◇◇

On an individual level, start to get to know the people around you. What do they like to do outside of work? Do they have families? What are their interests, hobbies? What events are going on in their lives? Share stories. A good place to start is to ask people about their weekend plans when Friday is winding down. Try it this week, and see how it goes.

I think this technique works especially well on those coworkers you have labeled as "difficult" (you know you have) either because of their personalities or poor work performances (see Emerald #6). Chances are, you have only dealt with those people on a business or task level, and perhaps for good reason. But if you were to ask about their outside interests, you might just be surprised at how they warm up to you. People love to talk about themselves and feel appreciated. By giving those folks the cold shoulder, you only make the problem worse. You make no headway, they continue to feel alienated, and become ever more "difficult."

Lead with empathy. When you know coworkers better, you get a better handle on their external circumstances. When this happens, you can be more understanding of and flexible to their needs. Research shows that we do not give credit to people for their external circumstances the way we do ourselves.[10] We understand that *we* have a lot of outside pressures, but we often do not extend this courtesy of understanding to other people.

I think some people take this courtesy of understanding to mean that you need to be "touchy-feely" on the one hand or "nosey" on the other. What I am referring to does not come close to either of those extremes. But you do have to make your employees feel like they can come to you with some of their "life" issues. If you know some of the basics about your coworkers' lives, you can adjust workloads accordingly.

My husband once had to have emergency knee surgery. The word "emergency" should tell you it was unplanned! Well, it threw our world into chaos for the next month.

If you were my boss, and you knew about the situation, you could maybe ease the burden on me for a while, and I would be appreciative. If you expected me to carry on as usual with "no excuses," whether you knew about the situation or not, I would be resentful. Now, I would not expect you to completely re-vamp work processes to accommodate my situation, but a little empathy would be nice. Maybe we could work on a solution together.

It also makes good business sense when you can tailor processes to people because you understand their preferences for working. You can rest assured in giving employees autonomy because they have designed personalized game plans for success.

On a group or organizational level, hold informal gatherings where no shop talk is allowed. Let people form bonds. It is, after all, the *people* your employees work with that make them want to stay at a job. Give some thought to the idea of building a workplace where people want to come to everyday. Work to create a nurturing space where people feel welcomed and able to bring their whole selves to work.

You would need to create this space on multiple levels. Think about the physical environment: is it bright, cheery, welcoming? How about the workers' physical movement as they do their work: is it too limiting or too strenuous? Move on to the mental aspects: do people feel challenged, engaged? You have to do things to get their minds in full gear. Then address the emotional side: do they feel upbeat and passionate about the work, or are they frustrated and defeated?

As you stand back to look at the wider organizational picture, you can see whether people's whole range of needs are being fulfilled. What is the organization doing or not doing that is holding people back from bringing their whole selves to the job? Once you answer that question, you can begin to build a more nurturing workplace where people *want* to be.

Wouldn't it be interesting to have a workplace where people like to escape *to* rather than escape *from*? Imagine how great it would be to have whole people, fully engaged in their work, pulling together to achieve your company's mission. I have one word for you: unstoppable.

Ruby Reflections

The top three most relevant rubies to me:

1.

2.

3.

Corresponding action plans I will implement:

1.

2.

3.

Obstacles to implementing action plans:

1.

2.

3.

Ways I will overcome obstacles:

1.

2.

3.

Better motivation will be evident when:

1.

2.

3.

Ruby Notes

[1] Grube, J. A., and Piliavin, J. A., "Role Identity, Organizational Experiences, and Volunteer Performance. *Personality & Social Psychology Bulletin*, 2000, *26*, 1108-1119.

[2] Morgan, J. M. and others, "Tales from the Fields: Sources of Employee Identification in Agribusiness." *Management Communication Quarterly*, 2004, *17*, 360-395. (Morgan is my maiden name.)

[3] Brown, M. H. "Sense Making and Narrative Forms: Reality Construction in Organizations. In L. Thayer (Ed.), *Organizational Communication: Emerging Perspectives*. Norwood, NJ: Ablex, 1987, pp. 71-84.

[4] See James Kouzes and Barry Posner's *Encouraging the Heart: A Leader's Guide to Rewarding and Recognizing Others* (San Francisco, CA: Jossey-Bass, 2003) for strategies on delivering recognition.

[5] Savishinsky, J., "The Unbearable Lightness of Retirement: Ritual and Support in a Modern Life Passage." *Research on Aging*, 1995, *17*, 243-259.

[6] Herzberg's (1959) long-standing theory that intrinsic factors (i.e., work satisfaction) are more motivating than extrinsic factors (i.e., money) was recently upheld in Bassett-Jones, N., and Lloyd, G. C., "Does Herzberg's Motivation Theory Have Staying Power?" *The Journal of Management Development*, 2005, *24*, 929-944.

[7] Christina Maslach identified these three dimensions in *Burnout: The Cost of Caring*. Cambridge, MA: Malor Books, 2003.

[8] See Bob Nelson's *1001 Ways to Energize Employees* (New York: Workman, 1997) for suggestions on how to reinvigorate a workforce.

[9] Fred Flintstone is a trademarked character of Hanna-Barbera Productions, Inc.

[10] This phenomenon, known as the fundamental attribution error, has been studied in the workplace by Martin, S. L., and Klimoski, R. J., "Use of Verbal Protocols to Trace Cognitions Associated with Self- and Supervisor Evaluations of Performance. *Organizational Behavior and Human Decision Processes*, 1990, 46, 135-154.

Leadership

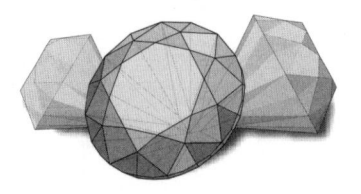

The Sapphires in Your Workplace

The beauty of the sapphire, with its pure blue sparkle, reminds of clear skies and still waters--brilliant and cool. Do those two words describe you as a leader? Do people see you as competent, level-headed, fair, approachable, understanding, up to speed, and up to snuff? Yes, that is a lot to measure up to, but it is important for yourself, your team, and your organization that you try to reach those expectations or even exceed them. You need to work harder than ever to win the support of the people around you.

Your leadership philosophy should revolve around a theme that is really quite simple: trust, respect, and care for others and they will trust, respect, and care for you. Trust them to do the work, respect their contributions, and genuinely care about them as human beings. The sapphires in your workplace will enhance your ability to lead others to success.

> If your actions inspire others to dream more, learn more, do more and become more, you are a leader.
> —John Quincy Adams

Sapphire #1

Let Go

Most people I talk to about their work want control over it. They want the autonomy to do things their way, within reason. People want to manage the things they are responsible for. They may not always go by the title of "manager," but they want the pride and sense of accomplishment that comes from seeing a project through from beginning to end.

Micro-managing kills the spirit. People do not want to feel like programmed robots; they want to make decisions that require innovative problem-solving skills to see direct, positive outcomes. If they are not able to flex their intellectual and creative muscles, they will feel devalued. When this happens, they might chronically complain, go numb, hide, resist, sabotage, or walk--pick your negative outcome(s).

So, here's the key: *trust* in your people's abilities. It is, after all, why you hired them. An executive director of a nonprofit agency, frustrated with board members for questioning his every move, finally told them: "You hired me to drive the bus, so let me drive the bus."

Give people the space and time necessary to bring their talents to fruition. I am always amazed when professional football coaches are fired after one or two losing seasons! It seems to me that there are a whole host of reasons for losing, and the coach is but one element. To fire someone before they have a chance to grow, or at least survive the learning curve, is not only unwise, but expensive.

One employee was fired after only one week on the job because his boss thought he was not learning fast enough "how things worked" at the organization. One week! What a waste of resources in time and money. I assured this person that he should feel lucky to have been let go from such a place. The employee had just left another job that had a "no re-hire" policy for people who quit. Ouch. The company's lack of trust in the employee's abilities was costly for everyone involved.

I once headed up a project that meant leaving the cozy confines of my regular routine, and it meant delegating and trusting people in new tasks. I worried about losing control. A colleague, hearing my worries, likened my delegates to kids: "Jayne, you just have to love them and let them go."

To let go, you must shake the notion that there is one right way to do something. I remember as a child giving up on learning to cook because my mother would constantly and urgently correct me if I didn't do things "just right." In my frustration, I gave up. The point is it doesn't matter if the batter is stirred clockwise or counter-clockwise; it will still produce nice, fluffy pancakes.

A woman who had worked in human resources reflected on how her boss had the faith in her to try challenging tasks. The boss was also willing to let her fail. The employee explained how the boss was always there for her, but in a "waiting in the wings" kind of way.

She mentioned a time when the boss trusted her, a neophyte employee, enough to speak in front of a judge in an employment case. The boss reassured the nervous employee she knew the case inside out, and could handle the high pressure situation.

The employee did not perform perfectly, but she did perform well. She perhaps didn't perform the same way the boss would have, but she performed to the boss' satisfaction. The confidence gained from that single event was immeasurable. From that moment on, the employee did not question her abilities, and the company benefited from her talents.

Another pitfall is the tendency for some leaders to overexplain work processes, to make sure every detail is covered. An employee in the nonprofit sector said he would rather be given the basics of a task and the desired outcome, and then he and his team could fill in the gaps to get it done.

When you map out the entire journey for employees, you are robbing them of their natural creative processes. In turn, you are being robbed of their talents. A group needs to work together, brainstorm, and get the creative juices flowing. When you completely take over, all of that is lost and it is *you* who lose.

The employees lose something too: they lose the *desire* to create something innovative for you. They will simply do what they are told, and that will be far from fulfilling for them. You can bet they will be checking the classified ads very soon for a better opportunity.

Let Go

Action Step

Use the principle of equifinality: there are multiple paths to a similar, same, or better outcome. Give people room to find the way and make it their own. You will be amazed at their ingenuity. Tell them how to get there and you will never innovate beyond your own, limited thinking. (Don't be offended--everyone has limited thinking.)

Now, not every employee arrives at the final destination. One manager explained that there were always a few people who didn't "get it," so she would give *everyone* on her team steps to follow. She did not want to single out the under-performers. When we discussed this issue as a group, however, participants decided that leaders must deal with poor performance issues one-on-one. It drives the "good" employees crazy when everyone is lumped together, or worse yet, brought down to the lowest common denominator.

A bank teller said her boss handed out a task list every week that basically described how to do the job. It was the exact same list every time, and had obvious steps on it like, "Balance your drawer." Is not the primary goal of a teller line to balance at day's end? If the tellers are not aware of this goal, there is a larger training problem that needs to be addressed. The teller said the list was for those few people who needed to have the job spelled out. It would have been better if the boss had worked with those few employees in private, trained them thoroughly, and left the rest of the workers alone to do their jobs right. When good performers are held up as the benchmark, the "few" become motivated to "catch up."

For good performers, let them chart their own course, or at least allow them to take detours. As much as possible (and this is the tricky part), *adapt* to your employees' modes of working rather than making them conform to your way of doing things (see Ruby #7). This approach can be difficult simply because you likely figure what has been successful for you will be successful for everybody. You probably have been rewarded for doing your job in a certain way, and all you know is your path to success (see Ruby #5). While it's good to *share* your methods with others, it's not always so great to *force* them on others.

Trust in employees enough to let them find the methods that work best for them. Let go, and let them do their jobs.

Sapphire #2

It *Is* About The Coffee!

It's the small things that matter to people. I was consulting with a group attempting to spearhead a culture change effort in their workplace. One committee member recalled how people used to make coffee for their co-workers. The first one in to work usually put on a pot so people were welcomed with the aroma every morning. But it didn't happen anymore.

They also used to have a system where people would contribute a dollar or so a week, and someone would go buy soda for the whole staff to drink anytime they wanted. Some higher-up decided it wasn't worth the effort or the expense anymore.

The problem is, the removal of "little things" wear on employee morale. (Did you like it when a bigger kid stole your toys?) Now, it may seem strange, because these are small (albeit caffeine related!) changes, but they mean a lot to people. Even the person on the committee who told this story thought discontent had to stem from something deeper than the lack of coffee. Then she exclaimed, after some thinking, "No, it *is* about the coffee!" Why? Not because of the tangible loss of something, but because of the SYMBOLIC message behind the loss.

When you take away the smallest of perks (no pun intended) from employees, it sends a myriad of messages that you likely do not mean to say: "You are not important," "We do not care about you," "We are stingy," "You are not worth the extra effort," "Get back to work," and so on. Okay, a boss might mean the last one. And people will get back to work. But will it be at the same level of work they had before?

It's a common problem. Sometimes the focus on saving money and effort obscures our ability to see the symbolism in our decisions. Sure, sometimes tough economic decisions have to be made, but think twice about the messages you are sending when you enforce those decisions. Consider the symbolic consequences as well as the material outcomes. The fallout from the symbolic impact may be more costly than the dollar amount you were trying to recover in your budget.

There are implications for any reward system you put in place. Be sure that you have the resources in time, energy, and money to keep it going (see Ruby #4). Once people get used to the system, and it becomes part of the organization's culture, people will cling to it tightly.[1]

There is a company who rewards all of their employees with a week's vacation to a tropical destination. They all go together on the company's dime. Granted, the organization has to reach an overall goal for the trip to take place, but heaven help them if they ever need to drop the program! I once discussed the impact of reward systems with a group of training participants. They agreed that no matter how big or small, reward systems that are put in place need to be supported over the long haul or they can backfire--badly.

You should also support "rewards" that arise naturally from informal interaction. In one of my workplaces, the salespeople would all gather around in the mornings to share bagels and chit-chat. It was often the best part of the day because the rest of the time we would be out "pounding the pavement" cold calling, and being served up hefty doses of rejection and animosity from the gate-keepers of the business world.

However, the boss thought that the "bagel ritual" (as I call it now) was a waste of company time. He thought we needed to get out and hit the streets right away. He didn't understand that those 20 to 30 minutes was a time for us to bond, bolster each other up, and find a way to get through the tough day ahead. When the bagel ritual was squashed, so were our spirits. What do you suppose that cost him in sales? Was the bagel ritual a "little thing"? It looked that way to my boss. Did it make a big difference in our performance? It certainly did. In making a decision that he thought would increase the bottom line, he actually hurt productivity and his profit margin because he failed to see the symbolic significance of his new mandate.

Think about your personal relationships. When it comes to romance or even friendship, people have long realized the significance of small gestures. Aren't you excited when a loved one actually *plans* and *executes* something meaningful to you? It might be a surprise birthday party or a special dinner. It might be a hot dog at the drag races. Sometimes the best gestures are the everyday ones. I am thrilled when my husband cleans the kitchen or goes to the grocery store without being asked to do so. Neither of those tasks is my favorite thing to do, and they always seem to be a burden. So when he does those things for me, the burden is lifted, even if for a short time. Is there a better gift to give someone?

The small things in the workplace are all about lifting the burden for a little while. People want and need small respites so they can be refreshed enough to carry out the work with creativity and enthusiasm. They also want to feel like they are worth the trouble. The combination of making employees feel needed *and* helping them with their work is unbeatable when it comes to maximizing worker contributions.

If a change in procedures is unavoidable, consider the impact change has on the "little things" people are used to. I consulted with managers of a retail store that went through transformational change. The changes were handed down from the corporate office; the managers at the local level had to comply. The company was attempting to move from a top-down to a bottom-up structure, where the front line employees would be empowered to make managerial decisions.

It was no surprise that the managers were not happy with the changes. One manager commented that she felt like a "glorified sales associate."[2] Not only did the managers' titles lose their luster, but their offices, and the prestige that came with them, were taken away.

During a change effort, organizations need to realize and recognize sacrifices people make for the process. Leaders can then take steps, if not to prevent, then to compensate for, the "little things" (which symbolically are not little!) that get lost along the way.

Action Step

Do not forget the SYMBOLISM embedded in the details. People actually do not require much to be happy but then do not take those precious few things away. One worker commented on how amazed he was about the crazy, positive response people showed when management showed up with ice cream bars on a hot day. Was it the treat that mattered? No. It was the symbolism behind taking the time and effort to get the treat that tells people that they are appreciated. And it goes way beyond food! Just think of all the little things that have a symbolic impact on your coworkers. Think carefully before altering or removing them.

Also think about little things that you could change or add to your workplace to make it better. I asked a group of nurses what the organization could do to help alleviate some of their stress. Several people commented that a particular machine in the nurses' station emitted a loud, obnoxious noise. It did not get used much, and did not need to be in the immediate area. Think of how simply moving that machine to a different space would lift the burden for those nurses.

Work to remove such obstacles to performance while building in other ways to help people out. Whether you alter, remove, add, or simply permit the "little things" to continue, ask yourself, "Does this (thing, event, process, ritual) lift the burden and show we care?" If so, go with it. If it compounds the burden and sends the wrong message, pitch it fast!

Sapphire #3

We Are Your PR Department

Your employees represent you and your company to the outside world. Most people who come in contact with your company for business reasons know the employees, not the top leaders (chances are). Ironically, it is often these front line employees who make the least amount of money, yet carry the greatest weight in representing your company to your customers. They could literally make or break you. Are they working as enthusiastic advocates for your business, or are they muddling through, or leaving a bad impression, or don't you know?

When I worked with a group of managers in a department store, they could all easily rattle off the corporate mission statement. But when I asked them what it *meant*, I received some blank looks. They managed to finally answer the question, but they responded in different ways. I found it interesting that they had never discussed as a group how to fill the slogan with meaning. I'm guessing the front line employees would also have no clue about the meaning behind the mission.

Even as employees may be short on knowledge about the company mission, they know full well how they are being treated on a daily basis, and will share this information with anyone who is willing to listen. Employees advertise your business to the world, for better or worse.

Think carefully about how employees are treated, and how they are *interpreting* their treatment (see Emerald #4). Even "little things" make a big impact. Workers at a bookstore said all they wanted was a chair to sit on when business was slow. The underlying issue here was not the lack of seating but the lack of concern for employee welfare. The workers were probably thinking, "They don't care enough about us to let us sit down once in a while!"

I, too, have endured the "no sitting" rule as a banquet waitress. I often seethed with resentment when I worked back-to-back weddings on a 14-hour Saturday, wondering how many times my bosses sat down that day. When I drove home, it actually hurt to step on the brake. I would spend the entire next day, my day off, with my feet up in the air, unable to do the things I wanted to do. Essentially, my workplace got two days of work out of me instead of one.

I was not happy about my over-controlling workplace. Did my friends hear about it? Of course. You obviously can't control what your employees are going to *say* about you or your workplace to other people, but you can take control of some of the issues in the workplace (which may seem small or trivial, like chairs) that they talk *about*.

Action Step

A few things need to happen here. First, your employees have to be educated about your business. You have to tell them what keeping customers means to you, and how essentially, it is they, the customers, who write the paychecks. The employees have to feel connected to the work of your business, and especially to the outcomes for the customer. They need to see how they contribute to making the customers' lives easier or better, more fun or interesting, and so on (see Ruby #3). There needs to be a level of excitement in providing that service. Simply put, there has to be something in it for them.

Second, people need to be treated right. It is extremely difficult to be treated poorly inside the organization and yet be expected to treat customers like royalty. I have talked with call center employees about this very issue. It is hard to experience negativity on one end of the line and then turn around and be "sunshine and roses" on the other.

People need to feel supported and connected in their work. When they are, and they enjoy what they do, that attitude will spread like wildfire, to customers and potential customers alike (and you never know when they are going to meet a potential customer!).

An employee stated that she was so proud of her workplace that when she drove home for the day, she would imagine the other drivers being envious and thinking, "Wow! She works *there*." How amazing would it be to have people thinking that highly of your company?

You have to consider whether coworkers spread the good word of the organization to customers, family, and friends, or air the company's dirty laundry and downfalls to everyone they meet. Do you even know? You better find out, quick! Take steps to make sure your house is in order on the inside so you can present a respectable face to the outside world.

Third, you have to make sure that there is a positive emotional charge to your workplace. This is not easy to achieve, I know, if it is not naturally there in the first place. If you get fired up about the work, however, it will be a lot easier for your coworkers to follow suit. You can't just try to cover things up with smiley face stickers and coffee mugs, however, or force fun and games on your employees in a negative environment. The "now we're going to have fun if it kills us" approach will backfire.[3] It will be considered, at best, cheesy, and at worst, manipulative. You must try to find the sources of the negativity and work to correct those first.

You can ask workers where there are problems, or simply listen in on a venting session or two. All employees have them, it's a club rule (see Emerald #6). Just overhear a few venting sessions and you will know exactly where employees stand. Do they feel misunderstood, unheard, under-appreciated, over-extended, or what? You will have to dig deep here, because what they complain about is likely a symptom, not the disease. It is usually not a surface problem, but a deeper issue of power, respect, or trust, that has coworkers spreading negativity.

Fix problems at the root cause, and people will appreciate your efforts. As your reputation *inside* the organization strengthens, so will your reputation *outside* your four walls gain steam. And as the company's image grows, the more your coworkers will be proud to brag about it.

We all know that word-of-mouth advertising is the most powerful kind of PR. You want it to work in a positive direction.

Sapphire #4

Be Good At Your Job

Ouch, this one hurts. But no one respects a leader who is less competent or skilled than the staff he or she leads. And yet we have all probably had a boss who fits that description.

The whole idea behind front line leadership is to "get in there" with your employees. Don't think of yourself as the lifeguard up in the chair where it's nice and safe, away from the choppy waters. True, you are valuable as a leader, but to earn others' respect, you have to show that you know and can do the work, and that you value the work done by others. Above all, you do not want to appear to be a slacker. Employees develop disgust for leaders who do not appear to be pulling their weight or earning their paychecks. A leader must find the delicate balance between doing and delegating.

The trouble is, normal leadership progression happens when someone excels in his/her given position, and is then rewarded with the title of "manager." This person is adrift in management, with little or no training on how to lead or what to do. The newly appointed manager then turns where? To the knowledge and skill sets that bred his/her success. S/he then instructs the team to use the same strategies. This fallback is natural, common, and yet, often ineffective.

If you were a star salesperson, and you become a sales manager, everything should be a breeze, right? Not necessarily, because people sell in different ways to be successful. Your team may resist doing it your way. The problem grows even larger when your span of control expands to include other specialties outside of your own. If you were a salesperson and now as a manager, you are responsible for the marketing department, new challenges will emerge. You might experience trained incapacity, whereby you know one segment of the work but have been blinded by the rest. Watch out for that steep learning curve just ahead!

If leaders have a sales background, they will likely stress numbers, quotas, percentages, and such. If they have an engineering background, they may be detail-oriented and focused on efficiency. If they have a creative background, they may emphasize the big picture and crave innovation. Having an angle of expertise such as this to leadership is not a bad thing, unless you fail to recognize and understand how other people's work styles and preferences differ from your own.

I was called in as part of a leadership training program to a company founded by scientists. They were a small group with Ph.D.s when they began the business. With rapid success came rapid growth, and the need to hire a whole host of non-scientific people to run the business side of the business. The scientists suddenly found themselves in management positions. They had to lead people from a diverse range of experiences, cultures, education levels, and expertise. The training was designed to guide them through the learning process.

The role of a leader comes with a (sometimes unwanted) shift from a specialist to a generalist position. Knowledge and skills have to expand proportionately. As your span of control widens, beware of the pitfalls. You lose a certain amount of "functional familiarity" when you oversee an ever-growing group.[4] You simply lose touch with how things work and how people are working together. It then becomes even more important to dive in and "get wet" from time to time, to regain a good idea of what is *really* going on.

Action Step

Learn the jobs of the people around you. Job shadowing is an excellent way to learn exactly what people do, what challenges they face, and how they interact on the job. Follow them around for a few days and ask a bunch of questions. You might disrupt normal functioning a little bit, but what you learn will be worth the inconvenience.

A symbolic side effect of learning others' work is that it shows people that you care about and value what they do. A technical side effect is that you will be able to spot inefficiencies that you can fix later. If it is not feasible to learn the actual skills in the job, make sure you at least *understand* what your coworkers do. You will be amazed at how adept people are at their work.

However, do not *assume* you know what your employees do (see Emerald #2). I once stepped in on an emergency basis to take over another person's duties for a three month basis (which, of course, was only supposed to last four weeks). When writing up the yearly report, I wanted to include everything that I had done for this position.

My boss told me there was no need, because he knew what I had done. The truth was, he did not know about all the demands of the actual job, from the learning cliff (not curve) I survived to the new computer program I figured out in one day, and so on. I made sure to write it all up so he could better appreciate my contributions.

Also be sure to practice what you preach. This sentiment is fairly common in the data I collect. People respect leaders who model the behavior they expect from others. A director of a human services firm wrote the following on a survey:

> One afternoon I was about to email my new boss a quick question, when I heard him chatting with the receptionist outside my door. Surprised that he was leaving early, I asked if he could answer a quick question. Later, I was "called" into his office and confronted about "not respecting his time boundaries." A week later, I invited him to meet my action team members during our monthly meeting. He and I agreed that he'd come for the first 15 minutes of the meeting. He arrived late and took 45 minutes of our remaining hour, leaving us short of the time we needed to cover the rest of our agenda.

Take stock from time to time to see if you are, in fact, following the expectations and standards you have set out for others to follow.

People become quite cynical when leaders take a "Do as I say not as I do" approach. People will, in fact, do as you do, *no matter what* you say. They believe your behaviors, not your words, reflect how you *really* feel about things, and they are watching you closely.[5]

Finally, take advantage of all the training opportunities you can. Hopefully your organization supports professional development. If not, see if you can persuade top management why it is important. If they still won't budge, seek it out on your own. Go to leadership workshops and seminars. Read books. Look! You are reading this one right now! Good. Keep seeking out ways to improve your leadership abilities.

I do not believe leaders are born. Sure, they may be born with an innate drive to lead the pack. But they are not born to lead the pack in such a way that inspires followership. To become the leader others want to follow takes learning and practice.

One test to see if you are the leader you want to be is to take a look at who is following you. Are they the stars of the organization? Are they yes-people? Are they carbon copies of you? Is that what you want? What *do* you want? Give some thought to the type and caliber of employee performance you expect, and formulate your leadership objectives and strategies accordingly.

Basically it boils down to this: do not lead from a distance, do your job well and set a good example. People will give you quite a gift in return--the results from *their* jobs done well. As a bonus, you will earn their respect.

Sapphire #5

Pick Our Brains

People want to help innovate and offer new ideas. In fact, you should really see innovation as part of employees' job descriptions. It is their *responsibility* to streamline processes, and to come up with better, faster, or easier ways to do things and make things. Do not suppress this activity for the sake of doing it "the way it has always been done" or doing it "my way." If you do, you will get exactly what you ask for--the same thing you have always had. Meanwhile, your competition is out there innovating circles around you.

A manager used a "boiling frog" analogy to describe how his former company had failed to innovate. He said that if you put a live frog in a pot of water and slowly heat it up, the frog will stay in the pot and eventually boil to death. Companies who are unable or unwilling to adapt to what the competition is doing or what the customer wants is like the frog in that pot. Compare this to a frog who is dropped into a pot of water that is already boiling. It will jump out immediately!

Leaders should consistently tap in to what employees are thinking and saying. The funny thing about brains, though, is that they need to be picked *before* they are ripe. People lose their zest for giving ideas very early in the process after being hired. In just a matter of weeks after entering the organization and offering ideas that are shot down, employees give up, shut up, and go with the flow. Companies (intentionally and unintentionally) wash out the originality of the person's ideas so he or she will better "fit" in the organization. However, a huge window of opportunity for innovation has just been slammed shut.[6] The next time you want to open it, you are going to need a crowbar and a lot of elbow grease.

When I was a new employee, I sounded like a toddler with all my questions of "Why do we do it that way?" I am sure I drove people crazy, and yes, newcomers can come across more obnoxious than helpful in the beginning. I would come up with suggestions for doing things differently and they would all be shot down, one by one. My favorite response was, "We tried that ten years ago and it didn't work." Good grief. At least think about the possibilities before closing something out. They could have at least thought about what was going on ten years ago when it didn't work. Then again, maybe the past doesn't matter all that much when it comes to innovation. What will work now?

When new ideas are not asked for, considered, or valued, employees will tire of hitting their heads on a brick wall. They will stop giving ideas and just do their jobs. Things will go back to "normal," which is to say, the same old thing. I know I gave up and kept quiet after a while. You know what? As I think back today, I don't have even the slightest clue as to what my ideas were back then! Washout successful.

With new and current employees alike, you have to provide outlets for innovation. Whatever approach you take, make sure you do *not* ask for feedback and then never look at it, or never take it seriously. People will become jaded, cynical, and resentful very quickly.

A retail employee said how workers were required to provide one suggestion for the suggestion box after each shift. Every eight hours of work they had to come up with a new idea and put it on an index card. Who can come with that many good ideas? Well, in the end, they didn't. The employees received no feedback about their ideas and, as far as they could tell, their recommendations were not being implemented. After a while, they began to fill out the cards just to fill out the cards and meet the requirement. They would write things like, "Get a new vending machine for the break room." The suggestion requirement was met, but it hardly produced ground-breaking stuff.

When you ask for ideas, take them seriously. Value co-workers' contributions. They are giving you a gift.

We also need to seek out diverse viewpoints to avoid the perils of groupthink. Just like individuals, groups can develop a one-track mind, where they expend a lot of time and energy pursuing a single solution. Innovation stagnates because other, possibly better, alternatives are ignored or dismissed.

An urban legend claims that during the space race, NASA spent billions of dollars in attempting to invent a writing instrument that would write upside down in the zero gravity and extreme temperature conditions of outer space. American engineers worked long and hard on a high-tech pen that would do the job. Meanwhile, the story goes, the Russian astronauts simply used pencils![7]

The moral of the (fictitious) story is that sometimes the best solutions are staring us right in the face, but we are too focused on looking in a different direction.

When we gather input from a number of people who hold different viewpoints, we have a better chance of considering multiple solutions. For that to work, however, people still have to be willing to let go of their own ideas. An idea is usually somebody's "baby" and s/he wants to keep it around for personal pride or validation or some other reason, but when something isn't working anymore, it just isn't working anymore. That brainchild is now an adult, and it needs to get a job and leave the house!

As a writer, I know it is very easy to become wedded to ideas. A lot of work goes into writing pages and pages of (what I think are) brilliant paragraphs! It is difficult to step back and think, okay, maybe they are not all brilliant. Or maybe, while good, some ideas do not advance the argument or fit the desired *result*. The next thing I know, I am pressing the backspace button, and whole, beautiful paragraphs lose their lives in the process! It is painful to erase all of that hard work, time, and creativity. But we all have to keep the big picture in mind and be willing to abandon a course of action when the *outcome* we need will not be met.

Action Step

Think about having people switch jobs for a few days. See if they can find work processes that are slow, unproductive, or downright idiotic in each other's work. Even when in their own positions, consistently ask employees to look for new ways of doing things. This system also works for new products or services that you want to develop. You have to make it clear that you want to know these things, and that is in fact part of the employee's role to tell you. I recently sat down with my boss to tell him about my experience with a new work assignment that was given to me. I told him of the challenges and offered a couple of possible solutions. I did this, not to moan or complain, but to simply keep him informed of the process as I saw it (as a newcomer to the role) and how I thought it could be better. I thought it was my job to tell him.

You could also formalize the innovation process, as long as it is not overly or unreasonably forced. Perhaps hold a contest or meet on a semi-regular basis, say, once a quarter, to discuss innovations. Reward those innovations with public praise. You want other people to catch the creative spirit too.

Even if you can't implement every idea, which you can't, tell your team that their ideas will be given careful consideration and a rationale will be provided for why they can't or won't be used. When turning down a suggestion, make sure the rationale is specific ("Steve is already doing that as part of his job") as opposed to vague ("That just wouldn't work"). When given a specific rationale, employees can tweak future ideas into something more workable. When given a vague rationale, they will stop contributing right there.

For new hires, get them in a room away from the rest of the employees and ask them about what they see and what they could change. Make sure you pick their brains no more than three or four weeks after they start.

Remember that big window closing? Use new people's fresh perspectives to your advantage. Do not be upset or offended by their suggestions, especially if you were the one who put the original processes in place. There is a natural tendency to suppress anything that looks like resistance.

Criticism is uncomfortable and ego-threatening. But counter messages are the very ones you need to hear (see Emerald #1)! Points of contention are points for change and improvement. If you are not willing to identify sore spots, your organization will continue to limp along and you won't even know it. (Remember that doomed frog from the analogy?) Your employees should be telling you what is going wrong. It is their JOB to tell you what is going wrong. Reassure your team you will *not* shoot the messengers.

Processes are meant to change. The dictionary definition of <u>process</u> is, "PROGRESS, ADVANCE: A natural phenomenon marked by gradual changes that lead toward a particular result."[8] Processes are *supposed* to change in order for something to move forward, advance. When a certain process was set up, it was done so in a certain context, for a certain time and for a certain purpose. Contexts change, and so must your processes if you want to keep the doors open.

People are valuable resources of ideas, and they want to be these resources for you. Tap in.

Sapphire #6

Yep, We Are Still Working!

File this suggestion under Anti Micro-Management: please do not bog us down in busywork that proves to you we are working. We are! That is, we could be, if we weren't too busy filling out reports that you won't read anyway. You care about results; we care about results. Let's focus on the end goal and not get too caught up in the micro-practices that get us there.

I was going along just fine in a sales job. We had a very flexible work schedule where we could set up appointments as they worked out for us. For some unknown reason, my boss decided to "clamp down" and hold us more accountable for every little thing. He did this by coming up with a points system. We earned a certain number of points per cold call, appointment, sale, and so on. The whole thing seemed ridiculous, because some days we just had fewer calls or sales to make than others. That is just the nature of the business. But "the nature of the business" didn't always look so great on paper, so you can probably guess what happened next. We fudged the numbers.

Another salesperson told me she ended up doing the same thing in her job (I don't feel so alone!). She was told to make a certain number of cold calls everyday, but she hated cold calling. I suppose nobody really *likes* cold calling, so that's why there's all the pressure to keep at it.

However, she thought the process of cold calling, where the chances of actually selling something are pretty slim (and the chances of getting a door slammed in the face are pretty good) was not the best use of her time. Instead, she took a relational approach to selling, and worked with those customers with whom she had built a rapport. But her boss only cared about the numbers on the report. He didn't ask, "What relationships do you have going on?" Instead, he asked, "How many cold calls did you make today?" So, she dutifully filled out the required report, fibbed on the numbers, and went out and sold the product her way. Guess what? She smashed the boss' sales record. Of course, the boss probably took credit for her success with his cold call report system!

Academic organizations are most fond of reports too. Every year, every faculty member has to compile a report on what s/he accomplished. Every group advisor has to do the same, as does each division, as does each department. Somehow this information all gets compiled into a massive book that proves, in fact, we have earned our paychecks. It is the craziest thing when you think about it. Our work should have been evident all year long. If we had not been teaching our classes, for example, I think someone would have noticed! And then, I wonder, who is reading all this? Or, at least who is reading all this with the fine-toothed comb precision with which we wrote it?

All of this time spent on these little things could be much better spent on, well, the actual work. One employee told me that he had to file his goals and objectives for the year with the higher-ups. Now, that doesn't seem too bad, except that he had to travel to a different city, along with the rest of the upper level salespeople, to *present* his goals in person. Because he had to take two days out of his schedule to go make the report, he nearly missed out on a very lucrative deal. How funny (or not so funny) would it have been if the goal reporting session prevented him from reaching his goal? As it was, the presentation was a major interference that did not need to be there.

The truth is, a lot of work that gets done is not visible, or not reportable. My husband would work until 1:30 in the morning to have product ready for the customer when the doors opened. But his efforts did not show up on a report anywhere. In the eyes of management, they did not happen.

Focusing on the measurable devalues the immeasurable.

In the medical arena, only what is reported on the patients' charts, counts.[9] What doesn't show up is the quality time spent with patients, explaining procedures, making them comfortable, and calming their fears. If it doesn't exist on paper, it doesn't exist. However, the process should be valued as much as the end result.

Action Step

Get out of your own and others' way. Always be asking yourself about desired outcomes. Take a big picture view: is the job getting done? Are the results you want coming about?

Question everything. For instance, why are we so hung up on having everything in writing? I suppose we have been used to the bureaucratic model of needing paper trails for so long now, we know nothing else!

Yep, We Are Still Working!

I should know. I come from the Land of Forms (a university). If there is a new procedure, then there will surely be a new form! In the move to a "paperless" environment we now sometimes use electronic forms. But then we promptly download and print out the form on, you guessed it, paper. We must keep the file cabinets full to capacity. It's state law.

Be like a toddler and constantly ask why you have certain procedures in place. Which ones are overly rational or red tape-ish? Work to reduce or eliminate anything that is a stumbling block. Organizations are moving too fast today, with all the changes in technology, competition, and customer demands. Internal processes simply need to be as slick and streamlined as possible. In a "lean" environment, there is no time for busy work.

Look at the *quality* of our work. Recognize all the effort that went into making it look so easy! Value the human contributions in the *process* of getting to results (see Ruby #4). See beyond the obvious, measurable things. Consider all the "behind-the-scenes" work too.

Basically, assume we are innocent until proven guilty. Until we give you a reason to suspect otherwise, believe that we are working, and working well.

Sapphire #7

Everyone Needs To Row The Boat

One thing I find consistently in the data is how people want quality coworkers. Specifically, people talk about how they want others to "pull their weight." How does this pertain to you as a leader? You have to make sure that they do. Employees become frustrated when their leaders are not assertive enough to hold everyone on the team equally accountable for the work.

The irony is, those people who *do* take accountability for their work usually get rewarded with . . . more work. I recently had a discussion with managers in a hospital about this very issue. Employees who do the job well will just get more work heaped on. Those who do not perform well are left alone and are given the least amount of work. Now, this condition wouldn't be so bad if the pay was different between over- and under-achievers, but usually, it is the same.

It starts to feel like the under-performers know something we don't! Their scheme is actually quite brilliant. As a leader, we ask you, please do not let them get away with it! Let your standards be known, and expect everyone to achieve them.

I took on some extra responsibility at work that involved learning a whole new position. After spending some time in the role, I thought that another person would be better suited for the job, for a number of reasons. Basically, I did not think it was the best distribution of resources to complete the task. I shared these thoughts with my boss. She didn't want to give the other person the job because she felt that the worker did not have high enough standards! I was thinking to myself, "Gee, you laid out your expectations pretty clearly for me, why can't you do the same for my coworker?" I wish I had said it aloud, but that's easier said than done. Instead, even though I was not the best fit for the job given my strengths, preferences, and expertise, I ended up with it because of my "standards."

See what I mean about the under-performers winning? They are quite clever (and perhaps don't even know it)!

On the other end of the spectrum, hold your "favorites" accountable too. Oh, yes, you will definitely have favorites; it is human nature. You are naturally going to like some people more than others (usually the ones who are most like you). They are probably people who perform well, but who do not necessarily go above and beyond. In retail and hospitality realms, the favorites usually get the best schedules. Many front line employees tell stories about hours being suddenly cut so "favorites" can have the prime hours or the most hours.

Because favorites are in good standing with the boss, it means that they, too, can get out of some work. When I worked at a country club as a banquet waitress, I would watch some of "the guys" just "hang" with the banquet manager, while the rest of us buzzed around them like a bunch of worker bees. If we stopped working to try and socialize too, we were reprimanded. It was maddening.

Action Step

Be consistent. If you are unhappy with someone's performance, have a one-on-one chat about what is going wrong, and what you expect to change. If s/he still does not change, then you can take punitive action. But do not ignore the problem and give the person less work or less hours, because that means you are giving your best people more work, and they will get sick of it.

I am to the point in my career, finally, where I feel like I can put my foot down. I refuse to automatically pick up the slack for the under-performers anymore. With the right leadership, I shouldn't have to. A lot of other people, though, do not put their foot down, and do the work they are given, but then seethe with resentment--not a good situation.

Your employees *want* and *need* you to stand up to the people who are not pulling their weight, because they are often not in a position to do so. An employee offered this suggestion to her boss:

> I would tell her to enforce the rules better and stick up for herself. Someone needed to be fired and she felt bad for her and kept putting it off. She always said stuff under her breath when people were late--never to their face. She always allowed people to make changes to the schedule, even if it meant she had to break her plans.

I know it seems weird and maybe even counter-intuitive, but people *want* you to uphold the rules. For every bad performer you think you spare by being "nice," you are alienating several more who are actually doing the job well (see Emerald #1). Do not make your star performers pay the price for your passiveness. Now, I am not saying to be a mean-and-nasty dictator type. You know that doesn't work either! Find some moderation. You can still be "nice" while making sure your standards and expectations are known to all and reached by all.

Yes, in-groups and out-groups are going to form; it's part of the organizational process. But do your best to make sure people are playing on a level playing field. It is all in how people interpret your actions (see Emerald #2). You probably do not intend to "play favorites," for example, but if people perceive you are, that's all that matters.

Proper delegation becomes important. Delegate to people based on their strengths, and as much as possible, their interests. I am not a detailed-oriented person, for example, but there are plenty of people (much to my amazement and relief) who are. Let me be in on the big picture brainstorming if you can.

You may need to get creative if jobs are fairly constrained by outside factors. Paperwork, for one thing, will probably never completely go away (sob). Then you should help people find ways to bring more of their strengths into the existing work. For some, it might be a creative outlet, for others, it might mean working solo more, or wanting to be challenged with a special project. Ask people what they want, and let them try new things from time to time.

Another issue is consistency. Avoid saying you are going to delegate, and then decide not to. Or, do not delegate for a time and then take it away. Delegation is a form of empowerment, and employee esteem is wrapped up in the project. When you take jobs away, you take away a slice of power in the process.

At my brother's house, furniture movers were hauling in a new bed piece by piece. My three-year-old nephew was basically in the way of the traffic going in and out of the house, so I gave him a task. I told him it was his "job" to watch when the men were coming toward the door, open it to let them in, and then close it behind them. His eyes lit up at the prospect of having a "job."

He was going along great when all of a sudden my seven-year-old nephew ran over to the door and opened it when the three-year-old was briefly distracted. When the three-year-old noticed that his door opener job had been crudely ripped away, he was NOT happy. He screamed and cried. The pride he felt in being the door opener was stepped on when the job was so forcibly removed.

Now, most of us can control the impulse to scream and cry, but if you have ever had an important responsibility taken away from you at work, you probably felt a lot like that three-year-old. The principle is the same whether we are three or 53. People gain a sense of power and pride when they have ownership of their work. They do *not* like to let go.

Conversely, do not hold on to all aspects of the job yourself until you realize you can't handle it and *then* push it off on people. At least that is how employees will feel, like you are pushing off the work.

An accountant told me of how his manager likes to take over all the details of a project. The employees are left with little to do, until they are forced to scramble when the manager panics that she can't get everything done. When in emergency mode, *then* she delegates. This type of last-minute leadership frustrates the whole team.

Keep the level of delegation constant, and make sure all the rowers are rowing. There will be a lot more smooth sailing for everyone.

Sapphire Reflections

The top three most relevant sapphires to me:

1.

2.

3.

Corresponding action plans I will implement:

1.

2.

3.

Obstacles to implementing action plans:

1.

2.

3.

Ways I will overcome obstacles:

1.

2.

3.

Better leadership will be evident when:

1.

2.

3.

Sapphire Notes

[1] See a discussion of Geertz's (1973) web metaphor of culture in Pacanowsky, M. E., and O'Donnell-Trujillo, N., "Communication and Organizational Cultures." *The Western Journal of Speech Communication*, 1982, 46, pp. 122-124.

[2] See my discussion of the role of language in change processes in Morgan, J. M., "Are We Out of the Box Yet? A Case Study and Critique of Managerial Metaphors of Change." *Communication Studies*, 2001, 52, 85-102. (Morgan is my maiden name.)

[3] Dandridge, T. C., "Work ceremonies: Why Integrate Work and Play?" In M. Jones, M. Moore, & R. Snyder (Eds.), *Inside Organizations*. Newbury Park, CA: Sage, 1988, p. 259.

[4] Schein, E. H., *The Corporate Culture Survival Guide*. San Francisco, CA: Jossey-Bass, 1999, pp. 108-110.

[5] When nonverbal messages contradict verbal messages, people believe and act on the nonverbal component as the "truth," mainly because it operates on a more subconscious, and therefore less controlled, level of behavior. See Leathers, D. G., *Successful Nonverbal Communication: Principles and Applications*. Boston, MA: Allyn & Bacon, 1997.

[6] There is a negative relationship, even after 6 months, between the amount of time on the job and the amount of innovation newcomers bring to their work. See Allen, N. J., and Meyer, J. P., "Organizational Socialization Tactics: A Longitudinal Analysis of Links to Newcomers' Commitment and Role Orientation." *Academy of Management Journal*, 1990, *33*, 847-859.

[7] While a good example of how we overlook the simplest of ideas in our workplaces, the story itself is a myth. See www.truthorfiction.com/rumors/s/spacepen.htm.

[8] *Webster's Ninth New Collegiate Dictionary*, Springfield, MA: Merriam-Webster, 1990, p. 937. (Yes, my dictionary is quite a few years old, but I am attached to it.)

[9] Diamond, T., "If It's Not Charted, It Didn't Happen." In K. Charmaz and D. A. Paterniti (Eds.), *Health, Illness, and Healing: Society, Social Context, and Self*. Los Angeles: Roxbury, 1999, pp. 196-206.

Conclusion

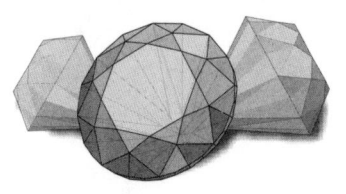

Discover More Treasures

Jackpot! The "X" marked the spot on your treasure map and you found what you were looking for. Or have you? No reason to stop here. You can add more gems to your collection by gathering insights from employees in your own organization. Use this book as a springboard for discussion, then dig around and see what else people are thinking and saying. You won't be disappointed, but you might have your eyes opened! When you gather new ideas and take action steps to implement those ideas, you will reap many rewards. Who knows? You might just discover the ultimate treasure you have been seeking: a satisfying and successful workplace, where excellent communication, extraordinary motivation, and exquisite leadership reign supreme.

Happy hunting!

About the Author

Dr. Jayne Witte (pronounced "witty") is a business trainer, speaker, author, and entrepreneur dedicated to advancing human potential in the workplace. She is Founder and President of Wits About You, a professional development business. She works with organizations in the service, manufacturing, finance, education, and health care sectors to develop human talent in order to achieve higher levels of workplace satisfaction and productivity.

Jayne is an Associate Professor of Communication Studies with a Ph.D. in Organizational Communication.

Jayne has authored several publications on the employee experience as it pertains to emotion, change, identification, and company culture. Her varied work background spans the worlds of sales, banking, retail, hospitality, and academics. Jayne uses first-hand research and experience to write about the common threads of workplace life.

A teacher of adult learners for 12 years, Jayne delivers interactive keynote addresses and training sessions on leadership development, communication improvement, and motivation contagion in the workplace.

Jayne is a bogey golfer--okay, a double-bogey golfer--but she remains eternally optimistic. She is proud to be a Jaycee, and volunteers her time to community service. Jayne shares her life with her best friend, husband Brian, and her second best friend, dog Sam.

POLISHED JUST FOR YOU!

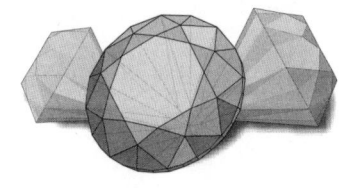

Jayne can tailor *Workplace Gems* for speaking engagements and/or training sessions for your organization.

Customization involves a basic poll of your membership followed by a consultation with an organizational representative. Based on member input and organizational needs, presentations can center on a few gems in depth or a touch on a broad spectrum of ideas for workplace improvement. Together, we can strengthen certain skills and/or create future action plans. The choice, and the voice, is all yours. Develop the "wits about you" and watch great things happen!

wits AboutYou
PROFESSIONAL DEVELOPMENT

www.witsaboutyou.com
jayne@witsaboutyou.com

SPREAD THE WEALTH!

Order additional copies of *Workplace Gems* to share with friends and colleagues! Special quantity discounts are available at ladderclimberbooks.com.

Workplace Gems _____ copies at $16.95   = $_____
Shipping & handling*   = $_____
Sales tax (7% --IA only)   = $_____
Total (U.S. dollars only)   = $_____

*Add $4 for the first book, and $2 for each additional book.

Name: _____
Title: _____
Organization: _____
Phone: _____
Email: _____
Shipping Address: _____
_____

❒ Check enclosed (payable to Ladder Climber Books)

Send to:
Ladder Climber Books
PO BOX 247, Cedar Falls, IA 50613-0018
info@ladderclimberbooks.com

Order direct at www.ladderclimberbooks.com!